JOHN CHEEVER

Literature and Life Series
[Formerly Modern Literature and World Dramatists]

Selected list of titles:

JAMES BALDWIN	*Carolyn Wedin Sylvander*
ANTHONY BURGESS	*Samuel Coale*
TRUMAN CAPOTE	*Helen S. Garson*
WILLA CATHER	*Dorothy Tuck McFarland*
T.S. ELIOT	*Burton Raffel*
E.M. FORSTER	*Claude J. Summers*
CARLOS FUENTES	*Wendy B. Faris*
GRAHAM GREENE	*Richard Kelly*
ERNEST HEMINGWAY	*Samuel Shaw*
JOHN IRVING	*Gabriel Miller*
CHRISTOPHER ISHERWOOD	*Claude J. Summers*
HENRY JAMES, THE NOVELS OF	*Edward Wagenknecht*
HENRY JAMES, THE TALES OF	*Edward Wagenknecht*
KEN KESEY	*Barry H. Leeds*
ARTHUR KOESTLER	*Mark Levene*
D.H. LAWRENCE	*George J. Becker*
MARY MCCARTHY	*Willene Schaefer Hardy*
NORMAN MAILER	*Philip H. Bufithis*
JOHN O'HARA	*Robert Emmet Long*
EUGENE O'NEILL, THE PLAYS OF	*Virginia Floyd*
GEORGE ORWELL	*Roberta Kalechofsky*
EDGAR ALLAN POE	*Bettina L. Knapp*
MURIEL SPARK	*Velma Bourgeois Richmond*
LIONEL TRILLING	*Edward Joseph Shoben, Jr.*
MARK TWAIN	*Robert Keith Miller*
GORE VIDAL	*Robert F. Kiernan*
ROBERT PENN WARREN	*Katherine Snipes*
EDMUND WILSON	*David Castronovo*
THOMAS WOLFE	*Elizabeth Evans*
VIRGINIA WOOLF	*Manly Johnson*

Complete list of titles in the series available from publisher o request.

JOHN CHEEVER

Samuel Coale

FREDERICK UNGAR PUBLISHING CO.
NEW YORK

Library of Congress Cataloging in Publication Data

Coale, Samuel.
  John Cheever.

  (Modern literature monographs)
  Bibliography: p.
  Includes index.
  1. Cheever, John—Criticism and interpretation.
PS3505.H6428Z6   813'.5'2   77-4829
ISBN 0-8044-2126-9 (cloth)
ISBN 0-8044-6081-7 (pbk.)

First paperback edition, 1984

For Emma Gray
who sees me through

I am deeply grateful to Nancy Shepardson, who typed the final manuscript cheerfully. To John Cheever, I owe one glorious afternoon and one superb body of fiction, without which this book could not have existed. I am grateful to Wheaton College, in Norton, Massachusetts, for allowing me a sabbatical to write this book. And I will never forget Greece, where I completed the manuscript—overlooking Mount Olympus, in a flood of Cheever-celebrated, ancient and renewing sunlight.

—S. C.

Contents

	Chronology	xi
1	Cheever's Life	1
2	"A Delicious Element to Walk Through"	11
3	"Other Haunted Cottages"	35
4	"To Bring Glad Tidings to Someone"	49
5	The Wapshot Chronicle: "Paradise Lost"	65
6	The Wapshot Scandal: "Such Eccentric Curves"	81
7	Bullet Park: "Lethal Eden"	95
8	Falconer: "The Invincible Potency of Nature"	107
9	Cheever's Art	115
	Notes	119
	Bibliography	121
	Index	125

Chronology

1912:   27 May: John Cheever born in Quincy, Mas-
         sachusetts, to Frederick and Mary Liley
         Cheever.

1929:   Is expelled from Thayer Academy in Milton,
         Massachusetts, for smoking and poor studies.

1930:   1 October: Publishes his first story, "Expelled,"
         in *The New Republic* as Jon Cheever.

1930s: First moves to Boston with his brother, Fred-
         erick. Becomes the literary protégé of Hazel
         Hawthorne, wife of Morris Werner, the biog-
         rapher of P. T. Barnum. Moves to New York
         City. Writes book synopses for MGM. Attends
         the Yaddo Writers' Colony, first in 1933, in
         Saratoga Springs, New York, run by Elizabeth
         Ames.

1935:   25 May: Publishes his first story, "Brooklyn
         Rooming House," in the *New Yorker*.

1941:   22 March: Marries Mary Winternitz, instructor
         of literature at Briarcliff College, daughter of
         Dr. Milton C. Winternitz, dean of the Yale
         Medical School.

1941–45: In the military service during World War II.
         Two years in an army line-infantry division.

1943:   Publishes first collection of short stories, *The
         Way Some People Live.*

1945–50:   Writes television scripts, including "Life With Father."

1950:   Moves to Scarborough, New York.

1951:   Is made a Guggenheim fellow.

1953:   Publishes *The Enormous Radio, and Other Stories.*

1955:   Teaches advanced literary composition at Barnard College in New York. His story, "The Five-forty-eight," wins the Benjamin Franklin magazine award.

1956:   Spends a year with his family in Italy. Moves permanently to Ossining, New York. His story, "The Country Husband," wins the O. Henry Award.

1957:   Publishes his first novel, *The Wapshot Chronicle.* Elected to the National Institute of Arts and Letters. Wins the National Book Award for *The Wapshot Chronicle.*

1958:   Publishes *The Housebreaker of Shady Hill, and Other Stories.*

1961:   Publishes *Some People, Places, and Things That Will Not Appear In My Next Novel.*

1964:   Publishes *The Brigadier and the Golf Widow* and *The Wapshot Scandal.* Spends six weeks in Russia on a cultural exchange program. *Time* runs a cover story on his fiction, March 27.

1965:   Receives the American Academy of Arts and Letters Howells Medal for *The Wapshot Scandal.*

1969:   Publishes *Bullet Park.*

1973:   Publishes *The World of Apples.* Elevated to the American Academy of Arts and Letters.

1974–75:   Is writer in Residence at Boston University.

1977:   Publishes *Falconer. Newsweek* runs a cover story on *Falconer,* March 14.

1

Cheever's Life

Not the details but the shape of the life and the character of the man arouse one's interest when speaking
about John Cheever. The story of his life, of his
achievements as a well-known writer, reflects in many
ways the American success myth. From a small New
England town he went on to become the author of
many heralded short stories in the sophisticated pages
of the *New Yorker* and from there to best-selling
novelist. His books have been translated into several
languages and his short stories have been anthologized
in the most prestigious collections of American short
stories. One of his stories, "The Swimmer" (1964), was
even made into a popular film with the same name in
1968. His career has been long and fruitful, and his
inventive imagination seems never to have deserted
him.

John Cheever lives in an old traditional house
(circa 1780) in Ossining, New York, one of those fashionable suburban hamlets that set the scene of so many
of his stories and novels. Cheever himself is a gracious
and delightful man with a wry smile and an infectious
sense of humor. The sharp and penetrating eyes are
often touched with the glimmer of cynicism and uncertainty, but the wry smile and the good humor are
always in evidence. He seems a part of the landed

gentry himself, walking across his several acres, along by the brook in the front of the house and over the wooded hill in back of it. The graciousness never leaves him, as if he were content with himself and with his vision of the world. His conversation is laced with religious imagery. He talks of the "miraculousness of the visible world" as if it were to him a deeply moving religious experience, and speaks of the "correspond-ences" between that world and man's own questing spirit.

John Cheever was born on May 27, 1912, in Quincy, Massachusetts, in a large Victorian frame house, which no longer exists, on Winthrop Avenue. His father, Frederick Cheever, was forty-nine years old at his birth and had a knack for story-telling and an eye for the ladies. He was a shoe salesman who traveled widely but who, after the crash of 1929, could no longer find work. In one of Cheever's first published stories, "The Autobiography of a Drummer" in the *New Republic* of October 23, 1935, John Cheever recalls the story of his father's life. The young shoe salesman begins his career full of enthusiasm: "I was more successful than I had ever imagined." Fate in-tervenes, however, and the once-prosperous shoe business collapses, leaving the older, sadder man full of bitter memories: "I was fifty-seven years old. I was growing old. I couldn't remember anything but trains and hotels and shoes." He is left feeling that his life has been a total loss, mourning the loss of "the world that I know how to walk and talk and earn a living in."

Cheever's mother, Mary Liley, was an English-woman who seems to have been gifted with the kind of modern business sense that her husband lacked. When her husband could no longer find work, she opened and operated a gift shop. In his short story, "Publick House" (1941), Cheever tells the story of a woman who has turned her home into a "Publick House, 1750." While the mother in the story is thrilled that she has been able " 'to arrange everything to look as old-fashioned as possible,' " the grandfather rages, " 'You've sold all my things. . . . You've made a business out of it—selling the past. What kind of business is that—selling the past?' " The son in the story, who has returned from living in New York for a few days to see his family, is upset at the changes that have taken place in the family homestead, at "an unnatural profusion of antiques in the hallway."

As a child Cheever was extremely close to his brother Frederick, seven years his senior, and relied both emotionally and financially upon him in Boston after his expulsion from Thayer Academy in Milton, Massachusetts, at the age of seventeen. The enduring intensity of the relationship between the two brothers —they took a walking tour in Europe together in 1929 and Cheever has referred to their relationship as a "Siamese situation"—can be traced in much of Cheever's fiction from the early stories—"The Brothers" (1937) and "Goodbye, My Brother" (1951)—to all four novels. It is almost as if Frederick helped supply a necessary stability and emotional reliance that young John could not find elsewhere.

Cheever's dismissal from Thayer Academy, ostensibly for smoking and poor studies, led to his first published story, "Expelled," in the *New Republic* of October 1, 1930, written when he was only seventeen. He sent in the story, signed it as *Jon* Cheever, and it was readily accepted by the magazine editor, Malcolm Cowley. The style of the story already reveals that precise observation and diction Cheever was to develop as an accomplished and well-known writer. He himself admitted that "since I started so very early, my style was well set before I was 21."[1]

In the story, he described and contrasted his view of the natural world outside the windows of the school, from which he had recently been expelled, with the dry world of academe inside the school:

I knew about the trees from the window frames. I knew the rain only from the sounds on the roof. I was tired of seeing spring with walls and awnings to intercept the sweet sun and the hard fruit. I wanted to go outdoors and see the spring. I wanted to feel and taste the air and be among the shadows. That is perhaps why I left school.

In the spring I was glad to leave school. Everything outside was elegant and savage and fleshy. Everything inside was slow and cool and vacant. It seemed a shame to stay inside.

Notice the decisive balance of his prose, the rhetorical repetitions and rhythms of "I knew" and "I wanted," and the balance and use of carefully selected words— "*sweet* sun and the *hard* fruit," "*elegant* and *savage* and *fleshy*," "*slow* and *cool* and *vacant*." The rhythms may be too obvious, drawing too much attention to themselves, but the beginning of Cheever's precise style is there.

Cheever went on to describe the regimented and dead system, as he saw it, of the preparatory school world—"Unemployment is a myth. Dissatisfaction is a fable. In preparatory school America is beautiful." Into this false environment he placed three characters: a colonel who comes to speak out against war (one of the most cherished of institutions at an academy founded by the "father" of West Point); Margaret Courtwright, an English teacher who is completely unaware of contemporary literature; and Laura Driscoll, a history teacher, who "dragged history into the classroom, squirming and smelling of something bitter" and is summarily dismissed. When Cheever was expelled, his feelings of exclusion seemed to foreshadow the later rootlessness and loneliness that would ravage most of his characters: "I have no school to go back to. I am not sorry. I am not at all glad." He concluded on a melancholy and beautifully well-balanced note: "Soon it will be time for the snow and the symphonies. It will be time for Brahms and the great dry winds." This strain of melancholy, this hope of spiritual and aesthetic renewal (the symphonies and Brahms) and this realization of unredeemed wanderings in a kind of spiritual exile or void (the snow and the dry winds), was never to desert him.

John Cheever may have been fortunate in his literary patrons. While in Boston he met Hazel Hawthorne, the wife of the biographer of P.T. Barnum, Morris Werner. She took him under her literary wing, and when he finally moved to New York in the 1930s supplied him with work to keep him eating. One of his assignments included the writing of the synopses of books for possible M.G.M. screenplays. His other major patron was Malcolm Cowley, the editor of the *New Republic*, a man who cherished and maintained such a role with other aspiring writers. Cowley recommended that he attend the Yaddo Writers' Colony at Saratoga Springs, run by Elizabeth Ames, a reprieve from the Hudson Street rooming house in which he was living in New York. Cheever maintains that he was not asked to stay at the colony after a month, because he was spending too much time at the nearby race track. However he did return there frequently as a kind of general handyman and factotum, particularly in the winters when he could spend his time with the servants or chop wood in the silence of his own company.

Simon and Schuster forwarded Cheever an advance of four hundred dollars for a novel, whose title varied—*Sitting on the Whorehouse Steps* and *Empty*

Bed Blues—but which never materialized. He continued to move in heady literary circles under the auspices of such men as e.e. cummings, Edmund Wilson, Hart Crane, and John Dos Passos.

It was again Cowley who offered five of Cheever's stories to Katharine White, fiction editor of the *New Yorker*, and in 1934, at the age of twenty-two, his first story was published in its pages. The *New Yorker* was first published on February 19, 1925, as a sophisticated and humorous weekly magazine. Today the early issues appear to be self-consciously striving for smartness, "chic," fashionableness and the shrill sophistication of the Twenties. The slick pen and ink drawings satirize the obvious targets of stuffiness and Victorian gentility. This image of an urbane speakeasy strives to create the atmosphere of a casually wicked, slickly elegant, urban arena of frivolity and fun. Since its inception it has published one hundred and nineteen of Cheever's stories; only John Updike and John O'Hara have appeared more often in its pages.

Thus began a long and close association that was to lift Cheever out of obscurity, assure for him a financially secure future, and lead to his achievements as one of America's foremost short-story writers and novelists. Although the relationship would falter when the *New Yorker* refused to print such lines as "I was wearing . . . chino pants cut so tight that my sexual organs were discernible," it lasted well into the 1970s.

Cheever married Mary Winternitz, a 1939 graduate of Sarah Lawrence College and an instructor in literature at Briarcliff College, on March 22, 1941. She was also one of the nine children of Dr. Milton C. Winternitz, dean of the Yale Medical School, and Dr. Helen Watson Winternitz, daughter of the man on the other end of Alexander Graham

Bell's first telephone call. The Winternitzes lived in fashionable elegance on Prospect Street in New Haven.

Cheever spent four years in the army during World War II. He later wrote television scripts for two years which included the popular "Life With Father." He moved to Scarborough, New York, in 1950, taught advanced literary composition at Barnard College in 1955, and spent a year with his family in Italy in 1956. In that same year he moved permanently to Ossining. The Cheevers have three children: Susan, who was for awhile married to the son of Malcolm Cowley; Ben; and Frederico.

Prizes and awards followed. In 1951 Cheever was made a Guggenheim fellow. His story, "The Five-forty-eight," won the Benjamin Franklin magazine award in 1955, and "The Country Husband" won the coveted O. Henry Award in 1956. Cheever was elected to the National Institute of Arts and Letters in 1957 and in 1973 was elevated to the American Academy of Arts and Letters, joining such other literary notables as Saul Bellow, Robert Lowell, and Thornton Wilder. In 1964 he spent six weeks in Russia on a cultural exchange program; the same year *Time* magazine ran a cover story on his career and his fiction (March 27, 1964). Cheever won the National Book Award for *The Wapshot Chronicle* in 1957 and received the American Academy of Arts and Letters Howells Medal (an award bestowed "once every five years in recognition of the most distinguished work of American fiction published during that period"[2]) in 1965 for *The Wapshot Scandal*.

When he turned sixty, Cheever suffered a massive heart attack and spent a long recovery period in the cardiac division of the Memorial Hospital in Tarrytown, New York. Following this he completed two

semesters as writer-in-residence, one each at the University of Iowa and Boston University. He then taught
writing for two years at Sing Sing, the prison in his
hometown of Ossining. In 1975, realizing that he was
fighting a losing battle against severe and chronic alcoholism, he confined himself for a month in Smithers,
an alcoholic rehabilitation center in New York City.

Cheever's battle with alcoholism and drugs has
only recently come to light. He has disclosed his addic-
tions to journalists in interviews published at the appearance of his fourth novel, *Falconer*, which was
hailed as "a masterpiece." [3] The alcoholism and the
heart attack seemed to intensify and darken his vision
of the world and at the same time to heighten his sense
of his own remarkable and near-miraculous recovery.
Once again he became a weekly churchgoer, finding
spiritual solace and sustenance in the liturgical ceremony and poetry of the Episcopal Church.

In a *Newsweek* article, Cheever revealed how he
had felt when he wrote his four novels. He was "very
happy" when writing *The Wapshot Chronicle*, "sui-
cidal" when writing *The Wapshot Scandal*, and "sick"
during *Bullet Park*.[4] Such feelings are reflected to
some degree in the novels themselves. The writing of
Falconer became the act of a man reborn and redeemed. He wrote the book in about ten months in an
unusually ecstatic and triumphant period of his career
following his victory over alcoholism. His remarks, in
a New York *Times* interview clearly express his recovery and the enduring religious and lyric center of
his fiction:

It seems to me that man's inclination toward light, toward
brightness, is very nearly botanical—and I mean spiritual
light. One not only needs it, one struggles for it. It seems
to me almost that one's total experience is the drive toward
light. Or, in the case of the successful degenerate, the

drive into ultimate darkness, which presumably will result in light. Yes. My fondness for light is very very strong and, I presume, primitive. But isn't it true of us all?[5]

John Cheever's books explore and trace the migration of the affluent middle class from the urban to the suburban realm.[6] The apartment houses on New York City's upper East Side provided the setting for the earlier collections of short stories—*The Way Some People Live* (1943) and *The Enormous Radio* (1953)—and the suburbs, the setting of the later ones—*The Housebreaker of Shady Hill* (1958), *Some People, Places, and Things That Will Not Appear in My Next Novel* (1961), *The Brigadier and the Golf Widow* (1964), and *The World of Apples* (1973). His fascination with and exacting representation of the manners and daily minutiae of this particular social class appeared early in the short sketches of 1943, in the fuller, longer stories of 1953, and remains with him still.

Cheever had always regarded the suburban scene as a focus for his art, especially because, as he himself suggested, it seemed to reflect and reward the aspirations of his own social class after World War II. His childhood in Quincy, a middle-class suburb of the more austere and patrician Boston, developed in him an identification with those social aspirations and provided him with an outpost close enough to the affluent and social hierarchies he both satirized and admired.

In the later stories one can recognize Cheever's expanding interests in genuine moral dilemmas and spiritual experiences that suggest a wider vision of life from which to explore and discover more lasting truths and values. His greater use of legends, myths, foreign landscapes, and biblical references in his books indicated this wider development of his art. Critics have suggested that instead of mere stories of manners he in fact created fables, parables, myths, morality plays, legends, moral allegories, and fairy tales. All these suggestions imply that Cheever was clearly and consciously creating fiction concerned with a wider vision of the world, that he was interested in creating a wider pattern of human experience than the suburban façade of his stories would otherwise suggest. Perhaps his determination to discover beauty and possible redemption even in the modern landscape had finally overcome his more superficial glimpses of that suburban landscape that had haunted him.

As a writer Cheever has been almost willfully neglected in critical circles. It may be that modern American fiction has consistently focused on social outcasts and anti-heroes. Cheever's suburban world obviously depicts a different class. Perhaps in our fascination with the underdog and his spiritual penury and aimlessness, we have lost sight of another world, as legitimate and as fertile as any for literary speculation and concern. To ignore Cheever's work would be to ignore a great deal of life as it is commonly lived in these United States in the latter half of the twentieth century.

If Cheever's vision of the modern world may at times seem narrower and more sharply focused than other writers, it may be because he cannot think of modern America in any other terms than those which apply to the suburban landscape. If he has limits as a writer, it may be more a matter of the way he confronts the experience of the modern world than in the particular landscape he writes about. It is time to take a long, serious look at John Cheever and his art in an effort to see just what he has accomplished and how he has accomplished it.

2

"A Delicious Element to Walk Through"

Cheever once remarked, "There's been too much criticism of the middle-class way of life. Life can be as good and rich there as any place else. I am not out to be a social critic, however, nor a defender of sub-urbia. It goes without saying that the people in my stories and the things that happen to them could take place anywhere."[1] However true this may be, the fact is that as a writer John Cheever has become closely identified with suburbia, those bedroom towns on the commuters' circuit along the Hudson River's east shore and those wealthy small towns in southern Connecticut just over the border from New York state. Most of his stories take place in the affluent, upper-middle-class bastions of Westchester and Fair-field counties. Here exist all the comforts of modern conveniences and modern living.

In his early sketches Cheever was very much the sharp observer of manners, the chronicler of urban and suburban social mores. For Cheever the suburban ex-perience also created a specific attitude in its in-habitants, a point of view from which to observe and judge the rest of the world. It also, however, was to become a condition of the soul, a spiritual outlook or understanding that came to epitomize modern man's alienated yet sporadically hopeful state. It is this deeper or broader concern that the later Cheever stories explore, a vision that lies beyond mere social chronology.

The Common Day (1947)

The story opens at a summer home in New Hampshire, where the Garrison family is staying, and traces the events of the day there. Mrs. Garrison, the owner and mother-in-law of Jim, the main character in the story, constantly bickers with her gardener, Nils Lund. At the same time the maid, Agnes Shay, hovers, over-protectively around Mrs. Garrison's granddaughter, Carlotta. Carlotta, spoiled and sullen, growls and spits at everyone who comes in contact with her. Later in the afternoon Ellen, Jim's wife, takes Jim to view an old dilapidated farmhouse, hoping that he will want to buy it. He, however, is not at all interested, and the episode leaves them both out of sorts with each other. Toward the end of the day, during the cocktail hour on the terrace, the gardener exclaims vehemently to Mrs. Garrison that she is no better than anybody else, even though she tries to pretend that she is by playing the role of reigning monarch at the farm. Thunder erupts suddenly, Jim catches a raccoon in the cornfield, and the day is over.

The story reveals the various frictions and social inequalities that exist between the Garrisons and their hired help at their New Hampshire farm. All the day's unpleasant events, however, have only ruffled the sur-face of this common day in the country, common, of course, to those fortunate enough to own big summer places staffed with servants. Nothing can really awaken any of the Garrisons from the conventional manner of the life they lead. They are insulated and isolated from any real human concerns or social matters, carefully organized as they are around such suburban social customs as cocktail parties and summer leisure. Despite the feelings of unease that ever so often bother them— the coons in the corn, the flies on the porch, the outburst of an occasionally over-wrought gardener— nothing changes. They seem ignorantly imprisoned in their own way of life.

We observe the Garrisons as prisoners of their particular social class. We see their inhumanities, their vanities, and their self-centered inattentions to one another. They are "common" only in their reflection of the suburban social set which they represent.

The calm and lucid style of the story reflects the basic calm of their way of life. The interrelationships between the characters are observed coolly and quietly, allowing the frictions and social irritations to reveal themselves unobtrusively. One might suggest that the style itself can be too closely identified with the same dispassionate manner with which the Garrisons view the rest of the world about them. The style and the tone with which the events of the day are carefully observed reveal only a careful observation of particular manners. No deeper insights into the human relationships are apparent. The story remains an example of the kinds of people and attitudes that are products of the suburban landscape.

The Wrysons (1958)

The Wrysons of Shady Hill are a perfect suburban couple. They believe in order, decorum, the social graces of the affluent middle class, and gardening. Each Wryson, however, has his own quirk or eccentricity. Irene Wryson dreams once or twice a month

about the explosion of the hydrogen bomb and visual-
izes an apocalyptic scene of a river retreat, hundreds of
people fleeing from the disaster in boats. Such a vision
undermines her belief somewhat in the comfortable
security of Shady Hill. Donald Wryson, her husband,
when depressed likes secretly to bake a cake. It reminds him of his mother and the security of his childhood.

One night Irene Wryson dreams her dream, suddenly awakens, finds that her husband is not in bed
beside her, and smells a strange sweetness in the air.
Can it be the sweet telltale smell of atomic ash? She
scurries downstairs and discovers her husband, who
has just burned one of his secret cakes. They stare
incomprehensibly at one another at four in the morning in the smoke-filled kitchen. Learning of their
eccentricities, her dream and his cake, they throw
the cake into the garbage and then "climbed the stairs,
more mystified by life than ever, and more interested
than ever in a good appearance."

The oddities they have just discovered about each
other they must quickly suppress to keep their suburban vision of order and "normalcy" intact. They
want to preserve and protect the conventional manners
and social rituals of Shady Hill at all costs. Their
glimpse of disorder and irrationality has frightened
them. Irene and Donald will take refuge in the "good
appearance" in an effort to keep the smiling aspects
of life in Shady Hill in place.

Cheever's observation of the suburban fear of
change and its submission to order and decorum is
clearly supported by the very manner in which the
story is told. In a sense the style abets the Wrysons'
temperament and manner, even though it appears to
be playfully mocking them. The calm and graceful
prose with which the story is told soothes the reader's

senses in its tidiness. The events of the dream and the cake pass before us placidly and dispassionately. The depth of the night's anxieties seems to be sacrificed to the beautiful calm which the style itself creates. It almost seems as though to Cheever the horrible reality of the bomb is no more frightening than the benignly eccentric habit of baking a cake in the middle of the night. We are left wondering whether or not the questions raised in the story and the anxieties revealed have not been too gracefully shaped and too easily passed over by the very style that has created them.

O Youth and Beauty (1953)

The main character of the story is Cash Bentley, a man disturbed by his thinning hair and advancing age. He was once a superb track runner and retains his charm and youthfulness. After every party in Shady Hill, when everyone has been drinking long and hard, Cash arranges the furniture of the house into an elaborate obstacle course and races headlong toward the imaginary finish line. After the broken leg that he received while racing one evening has healed, he runs the race again, much to his wife's alarm. He succeeds once again to everyone's relief, but still that does not satisfy him. The next morning he tries to race again, this time in his own home, and gives his wife a pistol to fire the starting shot that will send him over the obstacles in his path. She takes the gun and shoots directly at him, killing him instantly.

Cash could not admit that age was catching up with him. To do so would be to admit that youth and beauty are behind him. The obstacle races reveal his attempts to recapture that romantic essence and athletic grace of his youth that have always come so easily to him in the past. He has tried to transcend the natural laws of aging and in doing so has been brought down, dead in his tracks.

For Cash the suburban town of Shady Hill has always represented that very gracefulness of his lost youth. The beauty of life and the youthful atmosphere of the town have come to symbolize his own aspirations in his own mind. On a summer night his own attraction to the shimmering suburban scene and the youthful beauty it represents is revealed:

Then it is a summer night. . . . The passengers on the eight-fifteen see Shady Hill—if they notice it at all—in a bath of placid golden light. . . . Up on the hill, the ladies say to one another, "Smell the grass! Smell the trees!" The Far-quarsons are giving another party, and Harry has hung a sign, WHISKEY GULCH, from the rose arbor . . . the smoke from his meat fire rises, on this windless evening, straight up into the trees. . . . The air seems as fragrant as it is dark—it is a delicious element to walk through. . . .

Another aspect of suburbia has been revealed. It is a place of beauty and ease. Cash's mistake was not only to assume that such a place cannot and should not change, but also to believe that in identifying himself with the romantic image of Shady Hill both can and must last forever. In the story Shady Hill becomes more than a realistic location, more than a social setting of certain manners and customs. It becomes a symbolic representation of the youth and beauty that must forever elude someone like Cash, who pursues them relentlessly. The story finally reveals man's inability to live forever in the youth and beauty of his cherished hopes and longings, although these hopes cannot be forgotten.

This broader view of the human condition transcends the detailed reproduction of the suburban social scene that had long fascinated Cheever in his earlier tales. The pattern of romantic longing, of longing for some imagined perfect past and of seeing it embodied in the art of living in Shady Hill, adds a further dimension to the suburban point of view. Shady Hill appeals not merely to some deep-seated human need for security and social allegiance but to an ever-present desire for youthful simplicities and beautiful things. In "O Youth and Beauty" man's spiritual and aesthetic needs are revealed as being as important as his social needs. It is Cash's doomed pursuit of them that makes us realize how ineffable such things really are and how, even in suburbia, they cannot be prized and worshiped merely for themselves, as if time cannot pass.

The Housebreaker of Shady Hill (1956)

The main character of the story is Johnny Hake, a suburbanite who loses his job, experiences some financial losses, and one night decides to steal money from his neighbors, the Warburtons. He sneaks into their house at night after a party, finds Mr. Warburton's wallet, and escapes with nine hundred dollars. He knows that he has chosen a false path, that in his own mind he has now become a spiritual outcast within Shady Hill.

Johnny Hake is consumed by the guilt of his actions. All at once in his own mind the rest of the world reflects his own guilt, and he can see only a vision of corruption wherever he looks. Suburbia suddenly becomes a sinister realm to him, a reflection of his transgressions. At communion on Sunday, the stained-glass windows appear to him as "butts of Vermouth and Burgundy bottles." He thinks he hears

rats gnawing in the baseboard of the church and, becoming absorbed in that imagined sound, misses the
taking of communion. Suburbia, love, friendship, all
the decent things in his previous life, now seem fragile
and uncertain. How easily a breath can blow down this
flimsy framework of existence that he once thought
was so impregnable and solid! He prepares to leave
his wife, who has noticed the change in him, and
packs a suitcase for his departure. She, however,
rescues him from the railroad station, and he returns
home with her, more confused than ever. What has
begun as an act of theft and stealth has been transformed in his own mind into "a sign of moral death."
He has entered a strange, new realm where the battle
for his very soul seems to be raging relentlessly.

Johnny Hake plans another robbery and goes to
the Pewters' house in the dead of night. Suddenly he
hears a stirring in the trees, which turns out to be the
beginning of rain. The touch of the rain upon his
hands and face feels gloriously refreshing, and he begins to laugh. Almost instantly he is restored to his
former self. "No more than the rain" has redeemed
him, suddenly made him aware of the natural beauties
the world can offer: "I was not trapped. I was here on
earth because I chose to be. . . . What I did not understand, as I walked down Fifth Avenue that afternoon,
was how a world that had seemed so dark could, in a
few minutes, become so sweet. The sidewalks seemed
to shine."

Hake is restored to his former job. He replaces the
stolen money in Mr. Warburton's wallet. All is well in
Shady Hill once again.

What had happened to Johnny Hake? Certainly
he had sinned against the legal limits and the un-
written laws of friendship and community of Shady
Hill. But he had also sinned against himself, against

some inner moral sense of self and decency that would not let him rest. In effect he had willfully surrendered whatever spiritual innocence or honesty he had had. His own desire for personal comfort, his need for money to prolong and buttress his suburban existence, had resulted in a choice to commit not only an illegal act but also a morally contemptible one as well. For the trappings of suburbia he had sacrificed the very decency that that suburban landscape in his mind represented. The theft of Mr. Warburton's wallet had destroyed whatever sense of his own personal worth he had had, and he suddenly existed outside that benign framework within which suburban decency seemed to lie. In that moment when the rain falls on him, however, he regains his lost sense of values. He has been, in effect, baptized by the rain and restored to his appreciation of and respect for both natural beauty and suburban decency, as if the two were inextricably one and the same thing.

We have a tidy moral tale here. It is Hake who has been "reborn" while suburbia represents those moral standards from which he had strayed. Has this "rebirth," however, come too easily? If his foray into thievery were really determined and desperate, could his restoration have been accomplished so readily? Can the rain really wash away the sins of corruption so quickly and so completely? Did Cheever use Johnny Hake as an example of outcasts who, in rejecting the suburban existence, are in fact rejecting all that is good in the modern world? Clearly the suburban predilection for decency and honesty, accepted here directly and unquestioningly, has triumphed, and Johnny Hake has returned to uphold and be upheld by its middle-class virtues. However shady, the hill seems to have cornered the market on spiritual goodness.

Here is a tale about innocence lost and regained,

about the pressures of the suburban environment to appear affluent and decent no matter the price paid, about the modern world revealed as a corrupting and corrupted place. Johnny Hake is a man who has made the wrong moral choice and been exiled into a spiritual wasteland that can only breed more visions of corruption and personal retribution. We have entered a moral landscape, a place where good and evil are clearly identified, in which a man has consciously lost his way. These moral implications and patterns clearly suggest that this story is concerned with a wider vision of the world, of the dilemmas of human experience which transcend the suburban façade, than may, at first reading, be most readily apparent. This framework of innocence lost and regained and of the moral anguish and relief that accompany that experience underscores the best of Cheever's fiction.

The Scarlet Moving Van (1959)

A new couple, Peaches and Gee-Gee, arrives at the opening of the story in the suburban town of B＿＿, which is affluent and peaceful in the best suburban manner. Here the townspeople look upon discontent and unhappiness as a kind of infection which should be perpetually banished. The new couple's new neighbors, the Folkestones, out of courtesy and curiosity, invite them to dinner, where Gee-Gee gets incredibly drunk, gets out of most of his clothes, and rudely chants, "'I have to teach them, honey. They've got to learn.'" Peaches then admits that they've moved eight times in the last eight years, that Gee-Gee has consistently scorned all the social initiations and customs of the suburban towns they have lived in by getting stubbornly drunk and delivering rude, incoherent

speeches. He continues this socially damaging behavior and leaves within a year of his arrival in B_____.
The Folkestones are glad to see him go, feeling that
their self-contained, suburban environment has been
shattered and upset by the obnoxious Gee-Gee. Con-
formity to the accepted social code reigns supreme.
Out with all transgressors!

Before Gee-Gee leaves, however, Charlie Folkestone is granted a possible vision of the meaning of
Gee-Gee's carryings-on:

He felt he understood the drunken man's message; he had
always sensed it. It was at the bottom of their friendship.
Gee-Gee was an advocate for the lame, the diseased, the
poor, for those who through no fault of their own live out
their lives in misery and pain. . . . To the happy and the
wellborn and the rich he had this to say—that for all their
affection, their comforts, and their privileges, they would
not be spared the pangs of anger and lust and the agonies
of death. He only meant for them to be prepared for the
blow when the blow fell. . . . He spoke from some vision
of the suffering in life, but was it necessary to suffer oneself in order to accept his message? It seemed so.

Clearly Gee-Gee is the prophet sent to warn suburbia
that no matter what elaborate precautions are taken,
death and change are always victorious in the end.
For Gee-Gee suffering is, in effect, man's true spiritual
state and from this prophetic point of view to believe
in the everlasting grace and eternal comfort of suburbia is to believe in mere illusion. In order to maintain
that illusion, Gee-Gee must be summarily expelled
from the suburban realm.

Gee-Gee and Peaches move to another community
far below the social and affluent standards of B_____.
Charlie Folkestone learns that Gee-Gee had broken his
hip playing football a few days before Christmas and
goes to visit him. Peaches and the children have gone

to Nassau, and Gee-Gee is confined to a children's
wagon that he propels with his crutch. Charlie feels
that Gee-Gee is delighting in his role as sufferer and,
though a blinding snowstorm is beginning, leaves him.
As he leaves, however, he thinks to himself about
openly abandoning a friend in such a time of distress
and need.

That Sunday night when Charlie is safely at home
with his family the phone rings. Gee-Gee is in trouble.
He has fallen out of the wagon and asks Charlie to
come over to help him. He tells Charlie that " 'There's
nobody else. You're my only friend.' " Charlie, secure
in the comfort of his own family circle and aware that
the snowstorm is continuing in full force, hangs up
the phone. His conscience begins to bother him, but
he makes a drink and ignores it.

Charlie's decision dooms him. He goes right on
drinking. His wife consults the local minister for
advice, but Charlie accuses him of making sexual
overtures toward her. "In the end, he lost his job, and
they had to move, and began their wanderings, like
Gee-Gee and Peaches, in the scarlet-and-gold van."

Gee-Gee had gone on to call the fire department,
which came to his rescue in less than ten minutes.
Then he resumes his own disorderly life and has to
move from his community at the end of another year
once again.

Gee-Gee has threatened the suburban decorum
and becomes a permanent exile from it. Charlie, the
guardian of that social decorum, fails to help his friend,
is consumed by his own guilt, and falls from grace. In
both instances the suburban ethic has been found
wanting because of its strictly social limitations and its
spiritual deficiencies. The social structure, as upheld
by the Folkestones, is unable to make room for an
honest dissenter like Gee-Gee, however rude and ob-

noxious he may be. The spiritual deficiencies, as evidenced by Charlie's actions, include the sacrificing of the demands of friendship to the securities of the comfortable life. One is punished for being outside the pale, the other for being too much within it. In both cases the suburban manner and point of view have been stripped of their social and/or moral pretensions, without denying the very real material comforts which accompany and embody them.

The gilt and scarlet moving van, that shiny conveyance that "was an inspired attempt to disguise the true sorrowfulness of wandering," suggests both the good and the bad aspects of the suburban mentality. The van itself is beautiful and accommodating, though the color may suggest some demonic aspect of man's fruitless but inevitable quest. At the same time it is a symbol of impermanence and uncertainty. It may finally suggest the perilous existence of all men and the fragile dreams of permanence and comfort upon which the suburban "faith" is built.

The Death of Justina (1961)

The story begins when the narrator's wife's old cousin, Justina, comes to visit the narrator and his wife. Minutes after guests have left a luncheon, which the wife had organized in Justina's honor, Justina dies on the living room sofa. The narrator, whose name is Moses, finds that because of certain zoning restrictions, it is impossible not only to have Justina declared officially dead but also to have her body removed and buried. As the doctor tells it, " 'It seems that you not only can't have a funeral home in Zone B—you can't bury anything there and you can't die there. Of course it's absurd, but we all make mistakes, don't we?'" The mayor calmly explains that "'this is the world you live in and the importance of zoning can't be over-estimated.'" Moses, after pleading with the mayor, finally gets the documents from him to make an exception to the rule, and Justina is properly buried.

Throughout the tale the dignity and reality of death are carefully contrasted to the suburban social regulations, designed to deny and avoid that reality. Even MacPherson, Moses's boss at the advertising agency, insists that Moses must write a commercial for a glorified cure-all named Elixircol before he can go home and attend to Justina's demise. Moses writes a sharply satiric parody of an Elixircol commercial— "Does your face in the morning seem rucked and seamed with alcoholic and sexual excesses and does the rest of you appear to be a grayish-pink lump, covered all over with brindle hair?"—and hurries home. Justina receives proper burial, but it is not within the confines of Proxmire Manor. She is buried outside the boundaries of the town as if relegated to some city dump.

Moses attacks the undertaker and his helpers (in his mind) as would-be conspirators in their determined efforts to keep the reality of death from surfacing in the false sanctuary of the suburban landscape. The moral is clearly spelled out, as Moses recognizes the mistake that suburbia, as represented here by its undertakers, is making:

. . . aren't they [the undertakers] at the root of most of our troubles, with their claim that death is a violet-flavored kiss? How can a people who do not mean to understand death hope to understand love, and who will sound the alarm?

He returns to his office and writes another satiric and specious commercial for Elixircol, that false elixir of life which, like suburbia, exists to nullify the reality of death by avoiding it completely. Then he writes out the entire twenty-third psalm. Here is the old biblical truth, the voice of true prophecy. "The Lord is my shepherd," not Elixircol, not television commercials, not suburbia, not zoning boards. All these, promising some degree of immortality, are false. All these in avoiding the reality of death avoid the mystery and the beauty of life as well. They offer illusion in the place of truth.

The story begins with a personal meditation, a kind of thoughtful prologue, as if Cheever is speaking directly to his reader before beginning to recount the actual events of his tale. To Cheever in this prologue, the life his characters lead in contemporary times appears to be meaningless and stumbling blindly toward gathering chaos:

So help me God it gets more and more preposterous, it corresponds less and less to what I remember and what I expect as if the force of life were centrifugal and threw one further and further away from one's purest memories and ambitions; and I can barely recall the old house where I was raised . . . where all the books were in order, the lamps were bright, where there was a fire and a dozen bottles of good bourbon locked in a cabinet with a veneer like tortoise shell whose silver key my father wore on his watch chain.

Cheever went on to consider the role and meaning of fiction in such a world. He worried about the choices he himself has made as a writer and described those personal assumptions and beliefs that underlie his art:

Fiction is art and art is the triumph over chaos (no less) and we can accomplish this only by the most vigilant exercise of choice, but in a world that changes more swiftly than we can perceive there is always the danger

that our powers of selection will be mistaken and that the
vision we serve will come to nothing. We admire decency
and we despise death but even the mountains seem to
shift in the space of a night. . . .

The fact that some kind of truth or vision of life, some
meaningful pattern of human experience, will continually elude him and that only meaningless chaos will
continue to haunt him constantly worries him. The plot
of the story is then introduced as "one example of chaos"
that art is to triumph over, and the reader approaches
it with his awareness and response deepened and en-
lightened by Cheever's meditative introduction.

    When the story opens we see the narrator, Moses,
firmly rooted within the suburban social structure.
Suburbia is his world. He inhabits this particular
environment and must deal with it. Moses freely
admits, "When I abstain from sin it is more often a
fear of scandal than a private resolve to improve on the
purity of my heart . . . and death is not the threat that
scandal is." His encounter with death, however, is
about to engulf him.

    The journey Moses takes on his commuter train
back to Proxmire Manor, after leaving MacPherson's
office on the day of Justina's death, is labeled "a digression" that "has no real connection to Justina's death
but what followed could only have happened in my
country and in my time and since I was an American
traveling across an American landscape the trip may be
part of the sum." This admitted digression within the
story reveals the time and place, the contemporary
scene, of the story. The plot is not abandoned or de-
railed. It merely becomes the starting point or vehicle
for Cheever's wider ruminations, as if the moment of
Justina's death were a moment to contemplate the
whole of life and society in which she lived.

In this digression the story opens up to take all of present-day America into its consideration in the face of certain death. Americans seem to be caught in a restless migration, one that has not yet ended and that has produced only a profound disillusionment and disappointment. Proxmire Manor lures Moses homeward with "some private dream of homecoming," but the melting snowman "on one of the highest lawns" reinforces his own feelings of bitterness and disappointment. In the face of the stark presence of death, those routine customs and home-centered rituals of Proxmire Manor, as suggested by the melting snowman, the material comforts of the suburban life offer no spiritual consolation to the wandering commuter.

One other narrative device used in the story, besides the opening prologue and the digression, was the dream. In setting up the dream sequence, Cheever may have suggested the manner of his own art when he described "the strangeness of a dream where we see familiar objects in an unfamiliar light." He observed that "like any dreamer, I was omniscient, I was with them and I was withdrawn." Moses dreams of a crowded supermarket filled with the polyglot population of America. Customers are buying boxes and parcels, none of which are labeled, and are ripping them open at the checkout counters, where brutish men wait to push them out the door: "In every case the customer, at the sight of what he had chosen, showed all the symptoms of the deepest guilt; that force that brings us to our knees . . . beyond the door I saw dark water and heard a terrible noise of moaning and crying in the air." Moses's dream reveals a kind of judgment day for the consumer society, an apocalyptic day of doom in which customers are carried away outside the supermarket doors "in some conveyance that I couldn't see." The meaning is left purposely vague; the dream carries its own presentiments of doom.

Perhaps Cheever is suggesting that as unenlightened customers in search of the ultimate Elixircol, we delude ourselves forever and are destroyed by our baser instincts and other malevolent forces we cannot ever hope to understand or control. Only in trying to understand or contemplate death can we ever hope to understand life. If we do not, we shall be taken away and kicked out screaming and desolate into universal darkness.

Cheever's many narrative devices in "The Death of Justina" magnify that confrontation between suburbia and death, between the carefully zoned comforts of the material life and the terrifyingly limitless circumference of death. Such devices grow out of and transcend the rudimentary plot of the story, as occurs in several of Cheever's best stories. It is a magnificent accomplishment and demonstrates the variety of options the short-story form can choose to take. In this manner Cheever improved and extended the very form he himself had taken as his own, and he left it transformed and new.

The Country Husband (1954)

At first the plot of "The Country Husband" seems to be merely an assortment of random episodes. Francis Weed, the country husband of the title, is almost killed in a plane crash at the beginning of the story. He survives, when the plane crash-lands in a cornfield, returns home to tell his miraculous tale, and is confronted only by the usual family arguments and battles. No one seems to care very much about his escape from the jaws of death. Later he attends a party with his wife, Julia. There he recognizes a maid whose hair had been cropped in public—the humiliation meted out for living with the German commandant in occupied France many years ago. Then Francis falls passionately and ridiculously in love with Anne Murchison, the baby sitter. In the grip of this passionate attachment, he finds it difficult to maintain the social decorum required in suburbia, insults Mrs. Wrightson, a local social leader in Shady Hill, and fights with his wife. He seeks help from a psychiatrist and ends up comforted and appeased with woodworking as his prescribed therapy. On the face of it, this is the seemingly gerrymandered plot of "The Country Husband."

There is a deeper, broader pattern of experience, however, revealed in "The Country Husband." Francis Weed's narrow escape from death jars his sense of life. The normal routines of his life, which he has taken for granted for so long, are suddenly interrupted, and he recognizes swiftly the true fragility and precariousness that all life embodies. He returns to the elegant suburban community of Shady Hill with a reawakened sense of his own uncertain mortality and observes everything around him in this new, sensitive manner. For one thing he realizes the very real beauty that Shady Hill can offer:

The room was polished and tranquil, and from the windows that opened to the west there was some late-summer sunlight, brilliant and as clear as water. Nothing here was neglected; nothing had not been burnished. It was not the kind of household where, after prying open a stuck cigarette box, you would find an old shirt button and a tarnished nickel. The hearth was swept, the roses on the piano were reflected in the polish of the broad top, and there was an album of Schubert waltzes on the rack. . . . It was his element, his creation, and he returned to it with that sense of lightness and strength with which any creature returns to his home. . . .

It is as if against the black backdrop of his own imminent death, the light of such a polished world must shine miraculously brighter.

At the same time Weed realizes that the beauty of such a scene precludes intimations of death. Its very elegance seems to cancel out or override any deeper concerns and fears, as if it were challenging the entire concept of death altogether. In such a place his recent experience must necessarily go untold. Yet he has passed through that ominous brush with death, and the world around him cannot appear to him in the same innocent manner, in the same self-satisfied and contented way, that it had before. His vision of life and death has been transformed.

The usual routine delights of Shady Hill—old Mr. Nixon yelling at the squirrels in his bird-feeding station, Donald Goslin's overtly sentimental and self-pitying rendition of Beethoven's Moonlight Sonata on his piano, the Mercers' black retriever, Jupiter, galloping around the neighborhood—do not delight Francis Weed on the evening of his return. At the Farquarsons' party he recognizes the maid whose hair had been cropped and sees in her an emblem of human dignity in its most naked and socially exposed moment. The memory deepens his own awareness of death, his own deepened regard for the human condition, but it seems suddenly out of place in the social comforts of Shady Hill:

The people in the Farquarsons' living room seemed united in their tacit claim that there had been no past, no war— that there was no danger or trouble in the world. In the recorded history of human arrangements, this extraordinary meeting would have fallen into place, but the atmosphere of Shady Hill made the memory unseemly and impolite.

Shady Hill appears to him suddenly as a refuge and retreat from reality, a false sanctuary that can regard such a desperate display of human dignity as only an unseemly impoliteness.

It is after this realization that Francis falls desperately in love with Anne Murchison, the baby sitter. "The image of the girl seemed to put him into a relationship to the world that was mysterious and enthralling," and he was "struck by the miraculous physicalness of everything." Her image invigorates his own renewed sense of life's beauty, renewed as it is also by his awareness of ever-present death. He has passed through a dark night of the soul and is emerging, however foolishly at the moment, into an exaggerated sense of life's offerings.

Francis's vision, however flawed and comic, focusing as it does upon the unenlightened baby sitter, does strike at the heart of that state of spiritual grace and purity that Cheever could not help but admire and celebrate:

Up through the dimness in his mind rose the image of the mountain deep in snow. It was late in the day. Wherever his eyes looked, he saw broad and heartening things. Over his shoulder, there was a snow-filled valley, rising into wooded hills where the trees dimmed the whiteness like a sparse coat of hair. The cold deadened all sound but the loud, iron clanking of the lift machinery. The light on the trails was blue, and it was harder than it had been a minute or two earlier to pick the turns, harder to judge—now that the snow was all deep blue—the crust, the ice, the bare spots, and the deep piles of dry powder. Down the mountain he swung, matching his speed against the contours of a slope that had been formed in the first ice age, seeking with ardor some simplicity of feeling and circumstance.

Here may be the heart of Cheever's own vision of the world, a physical and spiritual moment of grace and beauty.

Francis Weed's romanticized view of his surroundings clashes with the realities of those surroundings. At the train station on his way to work, he notices a woman in the window of a passing train and imagines her to be a vision of Venus combing her golden hair. It is at this moment that his reverie is shattered by the loquacious Mrs. Wrightson on the station platform next to him. Francis insults the socially prominent Mrs. Wrightson, arousing later the fury of his wife: "Mrs. Wrightson runs Shady Hill and has run it for the last forty years. I don't know what makes you think that in a community like this you can indulge every impulse you have to be insulting, vulgar, and offensive."

Gradually Francis cannot abide this growing abyss. He feels cut off from the world he once knew and loved and is unable to cross the border into his new romantic world of passionate delight. His decision to seek finally the advice of a psychiatrist shatters his private self-esteem, but he admits to Dr. Herzog that he is desperately in love.

The plot of the story leaps suddenly from Weed's declaration of love in Dr. Herzog's office to a glimpse of him at some point in the future. When last we see Francis Weed, all seems back to normal. Woodworking has provided the cure: "Francis finds some true consolation in the simple arithmetic involved and in the holy smell of new wood." The suburban routines—old Mr. Nixon's shouting, Goslin's sonata-playing, and Jupiter's rampaging—continue uninterrupted. In Francis's vision the suburban world itself is restored to a world filled anew with possibility and delight.

Francis Weed realizes the precariousness of life

and of Shady Hill, that his suburban sanctuary may be more precarious than even life itself: "The village hangs, morally and economically, from a thread; but it hangs by its thread in the evening light." Shady Hill maintains its promise of a fragile beauty, no matter how unreal, precarious, and false it may appear to be at times. It may suggest escape and a false sanctuary, but it also is a realm of aesthetic delight and creature comforts.

Cheever recognized the constantly ambiguous character of his suburban landscape, and in the final lyric line of "The Country Husband" seemed to celebrate and comically castigate it at once: "Then it is dark; it is a night where kings in golden suits ride elephants over the mountains." Fantasy and promise, delusion and delight, balance each other in Cheever's vision of suburbia, the promise and delusion of permanent security, the fantasy and delight of beautiful comfort. Within that precarious balance the suburban landscape lies.

3

"Other Haunted Cottages"

Cheever's stories are filled with the carefully observed manners, emotions, and objects of the suburban landscape. These points of reference provide the stylistic texture, the realistic surface, of his fiction and suggest the themes of his work—middle-class uncertainties, an overall sense of loss and loneliness, a pervasive aura of guilt and self-indulgence. The style creates an urbane and skillful gloss or polish within which the zany absurdities of life can be viewed from a safe and careful distance. The effect achieved—a gleaming surface of carefully balanced and elegantly lucid sentences that make the world a tidier and more ordered place—even suggests a certain insulation on the writer's part.

In Cheever's darker tales objects often seem to overwhelm the characters' sense of well-being, as if these people were living in a strange and alien world of obstacles and mysteriously laid traps. Things suddenly appear threatening, disconnected from any meaningful pattern or experience. The atmosphere that surrounds them suggests a malevolent universe, unassimilated into man's desire for order and serenity. Cheever's manner of describing these objects reflects the spiritual rootlessness and unease, even fear, that his often aimless characters experience.

Characters themselves undergo strange transformations in Cheever's darker stories. The usual dispassionate tone of his style suggests a disinterested but sympathetic observer observing the habits and gestures of people he may know. The listlike shape of the prose suggests the manner in which these habits and routines are accomplished, one by one, carefully, decorously. Both tone and shape reveal the manners of the characters, the customs and ceremonies within which they lead their lives, and the kinds of customs and ceremonies they enact. When these customs are suddenly disrupted for no apparent reason, the fear of chaos threatens to overwhelm the characters' sensibility. A kind of demonic force or inexplicable terror seems to have abruptly shattered the superficial patina of their lives.

The Music Teacher (1959)

A man, the narrator, feeling that his life has lost its charm and his wife has lost interest in him, decides to take piano lessons from an old woman. This new hobby, he feels, will awaken his personal interests and take his mind off the dull routine his life has become. He learns to play a particular exercise on the piano especially recommended by the old music teacher. As he plays it at home over and over again, he begins to drive his wife to distraction. She is unable to stand the constant repetition of the monotonous melody and begs him to stop: "'Oh, not tonight, darling! Please not tonight! Please, please, *please* not tonight, my love!' and she was on her knees." From then on, she submits to his wishes, and their interest in each other appears to be magically restored.

Slowly he begins to realize the designs of the old

music teacher. The piano exercise has been calculated purposely to manipulate his wife into submitting to him, in order to make him stop playing it. Is the old music teacher in fact practicing witchcraft? He realizes the increasing nightmare into which he has stumbled. Strange new powers threaten to unnerve his rational suburban existence:

. . . he realized that he could not mention what had happened; he would not be able to put it into words. This darkness where men and women struggled pitilessly for supremacy and withered crones practiced witchcraft was not the world where he made his life. The old lady seemed to inhabit some barrier reef of consciousness, some gray moment after waking that would be demolished by the light of day.

The "witch" ends up mysteriously murdered one evening, and the light of day is restored. But these strange events seem to have opened a new and darker vein in Cheever's literary landscape.

The Seaside Houses (1961)

The narrator, a seemingly gentle and rational man (Cheever's narrators usually are), rents a cottage for his summer vacation with his family. He loves returning to the sea each summer, feeling that at the edge of the sea, life can renew and refresh itself. Yet at the same time he acknowledges the essential rootlessness and uncertainty of the human condition. However renewed, life still remains precarious: "The journey to the sea has its ceremonious excitements, it has gone on for so many years now, and there is the sense that we are, as in our dreams we have always known ourselves to be, migrants and wanderers—travelers, at least, with a traveler's acuteness of feeling." The immediate

feelings of joy and comfort he experiences at the shore
suggest the renewal of spirit that he thinks is to come.

He and his family begin to realize, however, that
the Greenwoods, who had lived there before, have
departed suddenly under mysterious circumstances.
Slowly, ominous portents appear. The words "My
father is a rat" are written on a corner baseboard.
Hidden caches of empty whisky bottles are discovered. The narrator learns from a neighbor that the
Greenwoods quarreled often and bitterly and that their
daughter, Dolores, had married because she was eight
months pregnant by a garage mechanic. The narrator
admits to himself, even though he has not known Mr.
Greenwood at all, that he can feel his disturbing
presence in the cottage "with uncommon force." One
night he dreams that he is an alcoholic, demanding a
bottle of gin aboard an ocean liner. He wakes feeling
that he has dreamed one of Mr. Greenwood's dreams.
Can it be that he is slowly becoming possessed by
some avenging and unquiet spirit?

The gloomy atmosphere of the summer cottage
slowly erodes the narrator's good-natured and rational
outlook on life. He grows irritable and decides to return to New York City for a few days. In a bar at
Grand Central Station he recognizes Greenwood from
some of the old photographs he had found at the cottage. Greenwood is definitely an alcoholic, and the
pain and the ruin in his face unnerve the narrator's
crumbling sense of equilibrium. He returns to the
shore, himself infected by Greenwood's collapse, ar-
gues suddenly with his wife, and abruptly leaves her.
When last we see him, he is married to someone new,
who dyes her hair orange and continually upbraids
him, and is in yet another seaside house in the summer.
His sense of security and happiness has been shattered,
and he remains an uncertain shell of his former self:

The lights from the cottage, shining into the fog, give an illusion of substance, and it seems as if I might stumble on a beam of light. The shore is curved, and I can see the lights of other haunted cottages where people are building up an accrual of happiness or misery that will be left for the August tenants or the people who come next year. Are we truly this close to one another? Must we impose our burdens on strangers? And is our sense of the universality of suffering so inescapable?

Suffering has taken root in his soul and will haunt him forever.

The straightforward and dispassionate prose of Cheever's style underplays the developing horror of the Greenwood legacy. Perhaps horror is too strong a word, since the narrator comes to live with his sense of loss and insecurity almost as decorously and mannerly as he once lived with his sense of renewal and hope. Nonetheless, the sense of developing menace and sinister malevolence is created by the underplaying style. The intimations of its lasting effects and possessive powers emerge slowly in the story. They seem to steal up upon the narrator, not precipitously, but gradually, as if the festering unwholesomeness of the cottage could take its deliberate time, aware of its own inevitable triumph. Even the name of the cottage, Broadmere, suggests the mysterious depths of the sea that are beyond man's comprehensive control and understanding.

Cheever worked the forces of nightmare skillfully into his realistic, daylight world by disguising them in that atmosphere of calm rationality that pervades his style. His apparent objectivity and calm are maintained throughout but only seem to increase the unhealthiness of the transformation. The almost demonic ritual of transformation works so well precisely because it is so controlled and calculated. Sinister forces, documented and shaped by the decorous and dispassionate prose, seem all the more sinister because of the inevitable manner in which they divide and conquer.

The Enormous Radio (1947)

The Enormous Radio has become one of the most anthologized of contemporary American stories. After purchasing a large radio, Jim and Irene Westcott discover that it is able to transmit all the voices and noises from the other apartments in their building. The radio itself is "like an aggressive intruder" with "a malevolent green light," and its presence intrudes upon the happy life that the Westcotts appear to be leading. The radio reveals to Irene, who listens to it furtively and obsessively, the seamier side of life: "She overheard demonstrations of indigestion, carnal love, abysmal vanity, faith, and despair." She is overwhelmed by what she hears and wonders if her own life could be so "terrible."

Jim becomes irritable, as if infected by the discord from the radio. He has the radio fixed so that it can no longer eavesdrop on the other apartments, but then it explodes. Irene wonders if the radio can now transmit to other radios in the building the sounds of the Westcotts' developing discord. He rails against her about her stealing her mother's jewelry, about her abortion—" 'You packed your bag and went off to have that child murdered as if you were going to Nassau' "—exploding her fond illusions that their life is as pleasant and decent as any life should be, better than anybody else's. Jim sounds like some kind of Old Testament prophet raging against the placid inadequacies of the life of elegant illusion. Irene, of course, is crushed. Through it all,

The voice on the radio was suave and noncommital. "An early-morning railroad disaster in Tokyo," the loudspeaker said, "killed twenty-nine people. A fire in a Catholic hospital near Buffalo for the care of blind children was extinguished early this morning by nuns. The temperature is forty-seven. The humidity is eighty-nine."

The voice on the radio, returned to "normal," speaks in almost the same disinterested and calmly carefree manner that Irene once possessed. The chillingly casual juxtaposition of the twenty-nine deaths and the temperature is reported objectively, dispassionately, and without concern, as if these items were each equally important. The "suave and noncommital" voice now contrasts Irene's present realization that life is much more painful and far less superficially decent than she once had thought. She is left suddenly aware of the discord and illusion upon which much of her own life has been built, while the voice on the enormous radio calmly chatters on.

The story, like many of Cheever's stories, tends to be written in a kind of episodic notation, moving from one glimpse, one incident, one bit of conversation to another. Incidents and objects seem to pass by swiftly in the almost strictly linear fashion of a list. The polished style reads briskly and quickly. The brilliant surface texture of the story remains luminous and almost deliberately casual, as if details and conversations, listed and overheard, are being set down as calmly and as objectively as possible. Here is the opening paragraph:

Jim and Irene Westcott were the kind of people who seem to strike that satisfactory average of income, endeavor, and respectability that is reached by the statistical reports in college alumni bulletins. They were the parents of two young children, they had been married nine years, they lived on the twelfth floor of an apartment house near

Sutton Place, they went to the theater on an average of 10.3 times a year, and they hoped someday to live in Westchester. Irene Westcott was a pleasant, rather plain girl with soft brown hair and a wide, fine forehead upon which nothing at all had been written, and in the cold weather she wore a coat of fitch skins dyed to resemble mink. You could not say that Jim Westcott looked younger than he was, but you could at least say of him that he seemed to feel younger. He wore his graying hair cut very short, he dressed in the kind of clothes his class had worn at Andover, and his manner was earnest, vehement, and intentionally naive. The Westcotts differed from their friends, their classmates, and their neighbors only in an interest they shared in serious music. They went to a great many concerts—although they seldom mentioned this to anyone—and they spent a good deal of time listening to music on the radio.

The paragraph reads succinctly, moves swiftly and deliberately, and summarizes not only the history of the Westcotts themselves but also the definite characteristics and values of their social class.

The tone of the opening paragraph is almost as objective and dispassionate as the voice on the enormous radio at the end of the story. What is unexpected and unsettling in the story is the change that Irene has undergone in her outlook on life. At the beginning she is no more than a statistic, the sum total of the bits and pieces of information that make up "that satisfactory average" of her social class. By the end of the story, however, her attitudes have changed. When we hear the final voice on the radio, its "suave and noncommital" tone reveals that casually precise and uncompassionate style she has outgrown. The reader, too, has become aware through Irene's "conversion" of the pain and discord of life, but the radio has now "returned" to that serene and careless objectivity that we have come to despise. It is as if Irene and the enormous radio are transformed in opposite directions, the one from illusion to the beginnings of understanding, the other from the revelation of much of the pain in life to the chilled and callous reporting of events with no understanding whatsoever. In both instances the radio remains "an aggressive intruder'" on the characters' state of mind and seems to have more power over them than they seem to have over it.

The Swimmer (1964)

One fine day Neddy Merrill decides to swim from a friend's house to his own home eight miles away by way of the swimming pools in the area. Neddy views himself as "a pilgrim, an explorer, a man with a destiny" in this suburban world, eager to celebrate the very beauty of that world by swimming from pool to pool on a beautiful summer day. Neddy's swim is intended not only for his natural pleasure but also as his personal tribute to the comfortable and elegant suburban realm and ideal, the general beneficence of suburban living, which he admires around him.

The voyage begins. He leaves the Westerhazy, where his journey has begun, and goes to the Grahams, who greet him warmly upon his arrival there. He decides to name his suburban "river" after his wife, Lucinda. He passes on to the Hammers' pool, the Lears', the Howlands', and arrives at the Bunkers' in the middle of a party. All the while his feelings for the beauty of the suburban surroundings are growing and expanding.

At the Bunkers' party he accepts a gin and tonic, after his swim in the pool, and goes on to the Levys' house. The natural scene continues to delight him, even when he hears the thunder of an approaching

storm. The rain comes. He stays in the Levys' gazebo
to watch it pass. At the Welchers' house he notices
that their pool is dry, a strange occurrence in the
summer. In front of their house he sees a For Sale
sign nailed to a tree. He cannot recall their having
decided to sell their house and wonders momentarily
if his memory could be playing tricks on him.

The voyage continues, but its nature changes. As
he crosses the street to get to the next pool on his
journey, someone tosses a beer can at him from a
passing car. He realizes at that moment that he will
not turn back no matter what happens but will continue with a determination that seems to the reader
suddenly strange and obsessive. His joke has become
suddenly more serious, his voyage some sort of personal enjoyment and delight.

He is shouted out of the chlorinated public swimming pool he comes upon, because he does not have
the proper identification disk. Mrs. Halloran, a possible
communist sympathizer who does not wear bathing
suits, tells him, after he has swum her pool naked, that
she is very sorry to hear about all his misfortunes. She
explains that she has heard about the selling of his
house, but he cannot recall such an action.

Neddy stops in to see Helen, the Hallorans'
daughter, and her husband, Eric Sachs, to get a drink.
He has noticed a definite chill in the air. Helen in-
forms him that since her husband's operation three
years ago, there has been nothing in the house to
drink. Neddy's demeanor is again shattered, for again
he cannot remember something as unfortunate as Eric's
illness. He walks in uninvited on the Biswangers'
party, a couple who do not belong to "Neddy's set"
and who have disrupted proper suburban decorum by
discussing the prices of things at cocktail parties and
by telling dirty stories after dinner to mixed company.

He is rebuffed by the barkeeper and overhears Grace Biswanger telling someone, "They went for broke overnight—nothing but income—and he showed up drunk one Sunday and asked us to loan him five thousand dollars."

The final rebuff comes from his former mistress, Shirley Adams, at the next pool on his list. The sight of him confuses her, and she questions whether he will ever grow up, and assures him shrilly that she will not lend him another cent. Leaving her, he sees over his shoulder a younger man who has obviously taken his place in her affections. Even love seems closed to Neddy Merrill.

The season has undergone a change during the voyage. An autumnal chill is everywhere. Neddy, cold and bewildered, begins to cry after all the rebuffs he has withstood. He swims the remaining pools, however, and heads for home. His own house is dark, deserted, and locked up. No one has lived there for a long time.

The startling revelation of the deserted house sheds new light on the events that have preceded it. Neddy's celebration of suburbia has really been a reaching out for things already lost, for time already past. His voyage reveals not only the beauty of the landscape, as well as the self-righteous and snobbish social hierarchy of the place, but also his expulsion from it. Financial reverses of some kind have exiled him in some way. In returning to recapture that sense of place that is no longer his, he realizes that he is an outsider now. He has been expelled from that beneficent world, from its comfortable surroundings, and from the social regulations that go with it.

Where has he returned from? What has happened to him? Cheever only hinted at the personal disasters that have befallen him—no money, no family, the misfortunes to which the naked Mrs. Halloran has referred—but the stunning truth of these disasters at the end of the story undercuts totally Neddy's own self-gratifying celebration of the suburban existence. Money and position dominate that existence. Without them all beauty rings hollow there. Neddy is now a mere wanderer involved in a perpetual journey; as far as his relationship to suburbia is concerned, he can only look backwards.

The dark empty house signified not grace and comfort but loss and desolation, and from that perspective the brilliance and natural beauty of suburbia can only be the galling reminder of some lost paradise. It is a false paradise, however, based all too obviously on money and social position. Neddy can celebrate the water and the sunlight all he wants, but disconnected from that suburban realm, of which he had been a part, they are too easily overcome by thunder and the darkness of that closed deserted house.

The developing recognition on the reader's part that all is not what it seems with Neddy Merrill and his voyage is carefully established by Cheever as the story moves on from pool to pool. The casual, calm prose, reflecting Neddy's own mind, gradually darkens as Neddy's memory becomes suspect. Beneath that lucid, almost lyric prose style darker moments intrude —Neddy's loss of memory, Mrs. Halloran's warnings, the gathering thunder, the autumnal chill in the air. The story begins to take on a dreamlike effect, as though Neddy were trapped in some ongoing quest that can only lead to some dark and terrible revelation. Cheever carefully laid the trail toward the deserted house, so that when the reader arrives there, he is stunned at the transformation that takes place between his first impressions of Neddy Merrill and his final understanding.

In "The Swimmer," Neddy Merrill has fallen from grace, but there is no restoration here. Suburbia may be limited in its moral scope and social pretensions, but outside its pale all remains darkness and dissolution.

╼╾╼╾╼╾╼╾╼╾╼╾╼╾╼╾╼╾╼╾╼╾╼╾╼╾

4

"To Bring Glad Tidings
to Someone"

About being a writer of fiction, Cheever once said,
"One has an impulse to bring glad tidings to someone.
My sense of literature is a sense of giving, not a
diminishment."[1] This sense of giving glad tidings suggests the comic or good-humored aspects of Cheever's
fiction. The curious episodes and patterns of our fre-
netic contemporary experience and the odd objects
and cultural bric-a-brac of our disposable contemporary society have always fascinated him. They provide
the materials for his fiction of manners, in which his
characters are always observed in the social roles
thrust upon them by the strict decorum of suburban
living. Cheever created characters who were trapped
in the often outrageous and bizarrely funny social
demands of the suburban brave new world. All of
this Cheever recorded meticulously in his even-
tempered, pleasantly ironic, and understated style with
the discerning but dispassionate eye of a camera.

The reader is always aware of Cheever's style, of
the way in which he describes his characters' actions
and dilemmas. People in his stories tend to be used
as examples of a particular theme or situation, such
as suburban social values, the moral pretensions of
the affluent upper-middle-class, or the often eccentric
happenings of chance that may occur unexpectedly to

them during the most ordinary of days. His stories often suggest that he is more interested in the carefully contrived outlining of overall situations than in the representation and creation of well-rounded characters.

Cheever seemed more interested in viewing situations from the outside, from a detached and distanced point of view, than from the inside, from a particular character's personal point of view. Such detachment accounts for the comic or humorous aspects of his style: to watch an old lady slip on a banana peel may be funny from a distance; to experience that slip from the interior point of view of the old lady herself certainly would not be.

One of Cheever's essential stances as a writer is as an ironic observer of the world around him. He observes and describes behavior, not the depth of feeling that may accompany it. From this often witty and determinedly detached point of view, he does not attempt to penetrate the darker and desperate depths of life but eagerly delights in the absurdities and arcane episodes of life. Cheever may often appear to be skating on thin ice in many of his weaker stories, but he delights in the intricate and filagreed patterns and designs he can create on the smooth, clear surface of that ice. The shapes and patterns of these episodes delight him—the inversions, unexpected turns, transformations, reversals, ironic twists—and often the delight itself, generated by his gentle ironies, becomes the most memorable aspect of the stories.

In the best of Cheever's stories he seems to be celebrating his own decorative language and "glad tidings," even in the face of (or perhaps because of) certain death and chaos. The reader, because of the quiet beauties of the prose, becomes aware of the artist's encounter with experience and with the materials of contemporary society and realizes that even within the boundaries of our throw-away, no-deposit, no-return world, genuine moments of spiritual renewal and natural beauty can appear. At the heart of Cheever's "glad tidings" lie these beautiful moments, these lyrical instances of calm and renewed hope. These rare moments of spiritual transcendence coincide in and with the presence of natural beauty, and the graceful lyricism of Cheever's style created and celebrated such occasions. We might call this Cheever's lyric vision.

This momentary state of grace often created in Cheever's characters the experience of spiritual elevation and moral uplift. At these moments his prose expresses their and his own personal emotions and sentiments, in the lyric poet's accustomed manner, rather than merely recounting external events. Such lyricism moves beyond the comic stance of the stories and into the realm of celebration. These moments come as the culmination of an ordered existence within which the universe momentarily exists, not as a mad poetic ecstasy, not as a strange mystical illumination. They are, therefore, moral, for they carry with them the age-old virtues that Cheever as a man and as a writer believes in—order, compassion, virtue, kindness. In Cheever's eyes, these alone can redeem the comfortable suburban landscape from its own spiritual deadness and self-indulgence.

A Vision of the World (1962)

The narrator, another one of Cheever's rational and sympathetic men whose tone is one of light irony and pleasant observation, is out one fine day walking in his garden. He responds to the beautiful day and salutes the smell of freshly cut grass and the corresponding memories of the promises of young love. Suddenly he comes upon a can buried in the garden. He opens it and finds a mysterious note inside. The writer, a Nils Jugstrum, has promised to hang himself if he cannot become a member of the Gory Brook Country Club by the time he is twenty-five years old. The narrator then spies a copperhead. The note and the snake interrupt his private reveries on natural beauty. For a moment he is shocked "at my unpreparedness for this branch of death. . . . I seemed to have no space for it in my considerations."

Later he goes to the supermarket to shop and impulsively asks a woman there to cha-cha with him to the piped-in music. She does, and both enjoy the moment immensely. On the way home he must stop his car to let a parade go by. He delights in the girls and boys he sees in marching formation.

At home his wife is undergoing deep distress about her role in life. The vicissitudes of her suburban existence seem to have reduced her sense of self and well-being, her own personal worthiness, to a state of perpetual blankness, numbness, and disuse. She feels, she says, like a character trapped in a television situation comedy. He tries to convince her that she is grieving not so much because of some deeply rooted sense of despair, as because her grief, in suburbia at least, cannot possibly be acute enough! They dine that evening at the Gory Brook Country Club. No trace of the desperate Nils Jugstrum can be found.

What our narrator discovers he most desires, secretly, is some kind of revelation that will "grant my dreams, in so incoherent a world, their legitimacy." What he wants is to find "not a chain of facts but an essence—something like that indecipherable collision

of contingencies that can produce exaltation or despair." He is in fact seeking a legitimate vision of the
world that will uphold the comforts of his suburban
existence and at the same time produce a permanent
state of spiritual certainty and physical well-being.

Several nights later the narrator experiences a
series of dreams, each indecipherable, each suggesting the possibility of that revelation he is seeking. In
each of the three dreams a totally incomprehensible
phrase is repeated. In the first he himself uses it in
replying to a waiter on a South Sea island. In the
second a priest or bishop exclaims it on a beach in
Nantucket. In the third a woman uses it in a cheer
during a game of touch football on a Sunday afternoon. The repetition of the phrase pleases him, for it
suggests that the discovery of some essence, however
mysterious, however untranslatable and unknowable,
is possible. The nonsensical language, the sound of it,
soothes him. The sensation of the constant repetition
of the meaningless phrase reassures him.

Sleeping in his seaside cottage on the coast one
evening, he dreams that he sees a pretty woman kneeling in a field of wheat. The beauty of his dream seems
far more real "than the Tamiami Trail four miles to
the east, with its Smorgorama and Giganticburger
stands, more real than the back streets of Sarasota."
She begins to utter that enigmatic phrase when he
wakes up to the soothing sound of rain. He thinks of
a farmer who will delight in the sustenance that the
rain will bring to his crops, of the plumber "who,
waked by the rain, will smile at a vision of the world
in which all the drains are miraculously cleansed and
free." And even lovers will be awakened by the sound
of the rain, that "will seem to be a part of that force
that has thrust them into one another's arms."

Then I sit up in bed and exclaim aloud to myself, "Valor! Love! Virtue! Compassion! Splendor! Kindness! Wisdom! Beauty!" The words seem to have the colors of the earth, and as I recite them I feel my hopefulness mount until I am contented and at peace with the night.

Here is the triumphant litany of the suburban visionary, the man who can delight in his worldly comforts and exorcise his guilt in the beauty of the falling rain. That delight may be all too easily founded on sheer sensation alone—the sound of nonsense, the sound of the rain—and it may all too easily eradicate the reality of death and pain in the world, but for that hopeful moment the delight evoked is real.

In the story Cheever's tone, style, attitude, and glimpse of spiritual and natural grace are perfectly in phase with one another. The lyric style celebrates as it creates the narrator's moment of visionary delight. Cheever's suburban vision of beauty reaches one of its highest peaks of celebration. Wisdom and beauty, the upholders of any man's vision, have here become one and the same, inseparable, in a kind of hypnotic chant of reassurance.

The Angel of the Bridge (1961)

The narrator of the story, once again, is one of Cheever's decent and rational men who hate the architectural wasteland of the present, miss the more familiar past, and yearn for a nonexistent simplicity in their lives:

The truth is, I hate freeways and Buffalo Burgers. Expatriated palm trees and monotonous housing developments depress me. The continuous music on special-fare trains exacerbates my feelings. I detest the destruction of familiar landmarks, I am deeply troubled by the misery and drunkenness I find among my friends, I abhor the dishonest practices I see. And it was at the highest point in the arc of a bridge that I became aware suddenly of the depth and bitterness of my feelings about modern life, and of the profoundness of my yearnings for a more vivid, simple, and peaceable world.

He coolly maintains his decorous ways and proper manners and is embarrassed by anyone, including his own mother, who blatantly reveals conspicuous enthusiasms in, to him at least, an undignified manner. The story opens in New York City with his mother waltzing on ice skates in Rockefeller Center in a red velvet costume with a short skirt. At once the narrator's squeamish decorousness and his mother's outrageous energies, for one who is seventy-eight years old, are counterpointed. The waltzing reminds her of her youth. For the narrator this behavior suggests only the eccentricity of age. His mother is also afraid of dying on a plane, we are told, another eccentric whim he cannot comprehend. Such delights and fears can only be odd incidents in the provinces of the old.

When he learns that his older brother, the certified "favorite" of the family, is afraid of elevators and fears that the building will fall down when he is in one, the narrator can only laugh. He cannot grasp the effect that an irrational fear may have on one's state of mind and health, since he himself has never experienced it. He is amazed at both his mother's phobia and his older brother's. They are only absurd delusions as far as he is concerned.

However, on his return from visiting his brother in New Jersey, he must cross the George Washington bridge and in doing so experiences a moment of fear and panic he can only refer to as "my spasm." The fear and panic are real. He suddenly must confront "my preposterous fear that the George Washington Bridge would blow away in a thunderstorm."

He goes to visit the family doctor, who only laughs and urges him to find some more courage. Next he goes to a psychiatrist, who urges a full analysis. He cannot afford the analysis and so decides on his own to see this irrational crisis through. Such fears simply will not do for this rational and orderly man. He almost loses consciousness, however, when crossing the Triborough bridge. Then he decides that the world is threatening, chaotic, and destructive.

His own fear is beginning to color his entire outlook of the world around him. Once more he tries to cross the George Washington bridge, but the seizure returns once more. Yet he will not give up. He will try one more time and decides to cross the Tappan Zee bridge. On the bridge the horrible sensations return. He decides that all is lost.

At this moment of his deepest despair, destiny comes to the rescue. A young girl, thinking he has stopped for her, opens the door and climbs in for a ride. She is beautiful, calm, and merry. She is carrying "a cardboard suitcase and—believe me—a small harp in a cracked waterproof." She is a folk singer and sings as he crosses the bridge:

She sang me across the bridge that seemed to be an astonishingly sensible, durable, and even beautiful construction designed by intelligent men to simplify my travels, and the water of the Hudson below us was charming and tranquil. It all came back—blue-sky courage, the high spirits of lustiness, an ecstatic sereneness. . . . I drove on toward the city through a world that, having been restored to me, seemed marvelous and fair.

She gets out of the car at the toll station at the end of the bridge and walks away, leaving him to drive

on alone but renewed. He is delighted by this "merciful intercession" and hopes that perhaps his mother and
brother can be saved in a similar fashion. But he
does not tell them about his experience because "the
harp—that single detail—threatened to make me seem
ridiculous or mad." He will preserve his rational decorum, his "normalcy," to the end. He will not push his
luck all the way and so refuses to cross over the George
Washington bridge. But the story ends as it began with
the narrator watching his mother skating, still going
"around and around and around on the ice." Her circular waltz completes the circular journey of the story.
Order and beauty are both restored.

    The "angel" of the story seems to represent that
same spirit of decency and hope that the narrator has
always prided himself on, that in fact has surfaced
before when he observed a mysterious hoop of light on
a plane trip:

. . . I knew I would never know if the edge of the desert or
some bluff or mountain accounted for this hoop of light,
but it seemed, in its obscurity—and at that velocity and
height—like the emergence of a new world. . . . It was a
pleasant feeling, completely free of regret, of being caught
in some observable mid-passage. . . .

The hoop, in fact, suggests an angel's halo. One could
almost suggest that the girl's beauty, her singing, and
her state of calm are manifestations of the narrator's
own "yearning for a more vivid, simple, and peaceable
world." She, as a manifestation of his own better
spirit, has appeared to rescue him from his fears, almost
as though he were rescued by that better spirit, im-
plicit and suggested in the beauty and manner of
Cheever's carefully crafted prose. The added touch
of the harp (not thoroughly gratuitous since it does
extend the ramifications of the "hoop" image) lends

the story a certain magical or fairy-tale quality that
may accompany such spiritual transformations.

Harmony is once again achieved. Restoration
magically occurs at that moment of deepest fear and
uncertainty. The human spirit has miraculously renewed itself. "Some merciful intercession," which is
embodied in the gently balanced prose of the story
itself, has lifted the narrator up from his darkest hour
and delivered him into the hands of his better spirit.
That better spirit, his angel of the bridge, has always
been as close by as that hoop of light and his graceful,
red-ribboned mother, waltzing in complete and perfect circles on the ice.

The World of Apples (1973)

The main character of the story is old Asa Bascomb, a
renowned and aged poet, who lives in Monte Carbone,
Italy. His most famous book of poetry is *The World
of Apples*, in which he lyrically celebrated the apples
and events of his childhood in northern New England.
As a poet, "he had created a universe that seemed to
welcome man; he had divined the voice of moral
beauty in a rain wind."

Bascomb had come to Monte Carbone to remain
anonymous and undisturbed. For him, the Italian landscape suggests ancient myths and religions and embodies that sense of life's true strangeness that he has
often celebrated in his poetry. In addition to this,
Bascomb is attracted to the old cathedrals with all
their sculptures and paintings. These art objects for
him highlight and embody the strange transformations,
the "marvels of metamorphoses," that take place as
life proceeds.

We first meet him in the story surrounded with

awards and prizes in his house. Yet he wonders why the Nobel Prize has eluded him. Bothered by this oversight, while visiting one of his favorite cathedrals, he comes across a young couple making love in the woods. This carnal vision suddenly overwhelms his poetic sensibilities completely:

It seemed to have more zeal and meaning than his celebrated search for truth. It seemed to dominate all that he had seen that day—the castles, clouds, cathedrals, mountains, and fields and flowers. When the nuns left he looked up to the mountains to raise his spirits but the mountains looked then like the breasts of women. His mind had become unclean.

Pornographic images flood his mind and spirit. He has succumbed to an obscene way of comprehending the world around him. He is stunned by this seeming revelation and writhes helplessly in the grip of it.

His maid, Maria, suggests that he make a pilgrimage to the church at Monte Giordano and have his thoughts cleansed. He decides to go and take an offering to the sacred angel there. Perhaps this will help him to renew his mind and spirit. The offering will be a gold medal awarded to him by the Soviet Union. At Monte Giordano the priest asks him if the gold in the communist medal is in fact pure gold. Bascomb is uncertain. But at that moment a ray of sunlight falls upon the medal, and the priest, seeing it as a sign, leads him into the small country church. There he offers his medal to the angel and gets down on his knees. That night he sleeps comfortably, and the next morning returns to Monte Carbone.

On his walk home he comes upon a natural waterfall in the woods. It reminds him of the Vermont of his childhood, and the memory suddenly floods his consciousness:

He had gone there one Sunday afternoon when he was a boy and sat on a hill above the pool. While he was there he saw an old man, with hair as thick and white as his was now, come through the woods. He had watched the old man unlace his shoes and undress himself with the haste of a lover. First he had wet his hands and arms and shoulders and then he had stepped into the torrent, bellowing with joy. He had then dried himself with his underpants, dressed and gone back into the woods, and it was not until he disappeared that Bascomb had realized that the old man was his father.

The memory delights him and he participates in the same baptismal ceremony his father had. He undresses, steps naked into the waterfall, and bellows like his father. At that moment he feels reborn, renewed, and reawakened to his former self. He walks home triumphantly, forgets about the Nobel Prize. "In the morning he began a long poem on the inalienable dignity of light and air that . . . should grace the last months of his life."

The linear precision of the style in which the story is written parallels Bascomb's spiritual crisis and restoration. Step by step the prose moves carefully, almost gingerly, as if recounting some ancient rite or ceremony. The dignified calm of the prose attests to the certainty of Cheever's attitude and vision and mirrors them both as perfectly as it ever has in any of his stories. The tone and lyric grace of the prose are in complete agreement with the tone and lyric renewal of Asa Bascomb's spirit. Style and substance, the medium and the message, are one in "The World of Apples." The deceptive simplicity of the story reveals the triumph of Cheever's fictional art and of his lyric vision, for both are finally inseparable.

Goodbye, My Brother (1951)

The scene is set at the Pommeroy family's summer place at Laud's Head, on an island off Massachusetts. The disruptive intruder on the otherwise happy Pommeroy reunion is the youngest brother, Lawrence, who has been away from them for several years. He is always observing the worst in everything and everyone around him. He reminds the narrator, his older brother, of a Puritan cleric because of his gloomy outlook and constant search for malevolent forces beneath the appearances of things.

The family attends a "come-as-you-wish-you-were" costume dance at the boat club. Many women come in wedding gowns, the men in old football uniforms. The dance, full of nostalgia and good humor, is a great success. Lawrence, of course, objects to such good-natured and innocent fun.

The next day after the dance the narrator and Lawrence walk along the beach, and Lawrence explains that he had only come to Laud's Head to say farewell to the family once and for all. His older brother is sick of his constant depressed and depressing outlook and tells him that such prevailing pessimism is really a distortion of reality. In his anger the older brother strikes Lawrence on the back of the head with a root. Lawrence is not badly hurt, and the narrator binds his wound with his shirt. That evening Lawrence, full of self-pity and reproach, rails against his older brother's actions. Lawrence and his family (his wife and two children have come to the island with him to join in the family reunion) leave for the mainland in the morning.

The narrator on that morning after Lawrence has

left observes keenly the beauty that the summer day
has to offer. For him, this is the true reality of life, this
almost lyric celebration of the natural beauty of the
world around him. In his own mind he poetically links
the aroma of the roses with the smell· of strawberry
jam. In the presence of such beauty, Lawrence's sad
and gloomy vision appears false and unrealistic:

Oh, what can you do with a man like that? What can you
do? How can you dissuade his eye in a crowd from seeking out the cheek with acne, the infirm hand; how can you
teach him to respond to the inestimable greatness of the
race, the harsh surface beauty of life; how can you put
his finger for him on the obdurate truths before which
fear and horror are powerless?

Lawrence clearly represents that New England
Puritan outlook that the narrator is trying to overcome
and discredit. The seemingly casual directness and
deliberate urbanity of Cheever's style itself undercuts
the darker seriousness of Lawrence's consciousness,
portraying Lawrence's pessimistic outlook as ridiculous
superstition when seen in the light of common day.
When stated so baldly and simplistically, the Puritan
ideas and observations on doom and mortality tend to
wither and look downright silly.

The purity and gracefulness of Cheever's style
capture that natural beauty of the summer's day. The
narrator glories in going swimming in the sea, "as if
swimming had the cleansing force claimed for bap-
tism. . . . We would all go swimming and shed our
animus in the cold water." The swim suggests an initia-
tion rite that allows one to participate in such a lyric
vision of beauty and serenity. It is the ceremony, the
ritual, through which one must pass to share this
vision. "The curative powers of the open sea," even
though perhaps an "illusion of purification," work

their magic on the narrator and on the reader. We are convinced of the reality of the narrator's celebration of natural beauty and of the unreality of Lawrence's morbid concerns.

Ritual is very important to the narrator. After he hits Lawrence on the head with the root and wishes him dead and buried, he adds, "not buried but about to be buried, because I did not want to be denied ceremony and decorum in putting him away, in putting him out of my consciousness." The exorcism must be accomplished ceremoniously and decorously to have any meaning whatsoever. In essence, the style, with its reassuring rhythms and calmness, its rhetorical purities and grace notes, and its lucid observations of natural beauty, creates that sense of decorous ceremony.

On the day of Lawrence's departure the narrator describes the vision he sees at the side of the sea:

The sea that morning was iridescent and dark. My wife and my sister were swimming—Diana and Helen—and I saw their uncovered heads, black and gold in the dark water. I saw them come out and I saw that they were naked, unshy, beautiful, and full of grace, and I watched the naked women walk out of the sea.

The final image, of course, suggests the rising of Venus from the sea. In Roman mythology Venus was the goddess of spring, rebirth, and love, and rose from the sea at birth. Cheever often uses many classical and Christian allusions and images in his stories. Their echoes add depth and resonance to his present scenes, as here the image of Venus rising from the sea broadens and strengthens the narrator's lyric vision as contrasted to Lawrence's image as a Puritan cleric.

The final image of natural beauty in "Goodbye, My Brother," redolent as it is with the innocence of nakedness, the rich colors of black and gold, and the reassuring and almost hypnotically repetitive rhythms of "I saw," creates and embodies Cheever's lyric vision. The lines create that moment, "full of grace," and establish that spirit of renewal and redemption, of rejuvenation and rebirth, as suggested by the sea and the classical overtones, that underlies the full-bodied lyricism of Cheever's best stories. The lines themselves can almost be written in poetic form, suggesting as they do the imagistic purity of much modern poetry, one image or event in each poetic line, simply and directly spoken:

> I saw them come out
> and I saw that they were naked,
> unshy, beautiful, and full of grace,
> and I watched the naked women
> walk out of the sea.

‿‿‿‿‿‿‿‿‿‿‿‿‿‿‿‿‿‿‿‿‿‿‿‿‿

5

The Wapshot Chronicle—
"Paradise Lost"

John Cheever's first novel, *The Wapshot Chronicle* (1957), begins and ends in the New England river town of St. Botolphs. The town has long been the home of the Wapshots, an eccentric New England family, the first of whom, Ezekiel Wapshot, emigrated from England in 1630. At the time the novel begins, the Wapshots living in St. Botolphs include the elderly Honora Wapshot, her cousin Leander, his wife Sarah, and their two sons, Moses and Coverly.

The novel opens on Independence Day. In St. Botolphs traditions are important, and the Wapshots are duly involved in the Independence Day parade. Moses and Coverly ring the bell at Christ Church early in the morning to alert the townspeople to the holiday.

Mrs. Wapshot can be seen seated atop the Woman's Club float. Since she founded the club, she gets to stand at a lectern on the float facing the charter members seated in folding chairs. Under the chairs is an Oriental rug. Everything would be fine, except that somebody lights a firecracker, spooking Mr. Pincher's old mare, which is pulling the Woman's Club float, and sets her galloping off up Hill Street. The mare finally comes to a breathless halt, but not until Sarah Wapshot's lectern has been overturned and

the whole town has been delighted by the procession
out of control.

On the night of the same July 4, the Wapshots,
while eating dinner at their home, West Farm, hear a
car crash outside. They rush out to see what has happened, and Moses rescues a young girl from the smol-
dering wreckage. Her boyfriend, Charlie, is dead—
they have made love on the beach that afternoon—but
Rosalie Young, the girl, recovers slowly and stays on
at West Farm. We learn subsequently that she is the
daughter of a clergyman, that she had attended sec-
retarial school, and that she had been but is no longer
pregnant, and fled from her home. She is drawn to the
peacefulness and quaintness of West Farm and the
Wapshots. This introduction of a new character into
the Wapshot household is bound to upset the routines
of life there. Leander, meanwhile, is trying to teach
his boys, Moses and Coverly, the importance of nature
and tradition in their lives, and Honora is going about
her daily rituals, slipping out to movies on the sly and
burning her mail which she does not wish to read.

After Moses has gone fishing in the far north
wilderness with his father, he decides to fish by himself
one day and comes upon Rosalie bathing in the stream.
He has not liked her—she reminds him too much of
his mother—but when he comes upon her in the
golden light of the forest and water, "he watched his
gleaming Susanna, shamefaced, his dream of simple
pleasure replaced by some sadness, some heaviness
that seemed to make his mouth taste of blood and his
teeth ache." (In the Bible Susanna is the young girl
whose nakedness while bathing attracts and excites a
group of elderly onlookers.) His sexual appetites
awaken. Adult desires and dreams have strayed into
the childhood sanctuaries of St. Botolphs. Honora

comes to the farm to look over the new guest, and while she is examining the contents of a closet, Moses and Rosalie come up the stairs. She overhears the consummation of their sexual longings. This is too much for Honora, who rushes home to read her Bible. That night she dreams of seeing spirits and figures dancing lewdly and obscenely in her room. The next day, so distracted has she become, she is advised by a stranger on the bus that she has left her dress unbuttoned.

Honora decides to sell the *Topaze*, the launch in which Leander transports vacationers from Travertine, the town in which the train from Boston arrives, across the bay to Nangasakit, where there is a beach and an amusement park. Then she suggests to Sarah that she take in tourists to make some extra money. Leander is outraged at her plans. Finally, however, Honora's real purpose rises to the surface. She announces that it is time for Moses to leave home and make his own way in the world. She decides not to sell the *Topaze* after all, if Leander and Sarah agree to let Moses go. Consequently, Moses prepares to look for a job in Washington, D.C., where some Wapshot relatives live. His parents celebrate his decision with a farewell party in his honor. After he has left, they discover that Coverly too, has gone to seek his fortune. Shortly after their departure, Rosalie is retrieved from West Farm by her obnoxious parents—her father, the minister, offers Sarah twenty dollars for having kept his daughter —and the summer in St. Botolphs is over.

The novel follows the adventures of Moses and Coverly in their attempts to find a livelihood, marry, settle down, and produce the sons that will insure their inheritance from Honora. Both Moses and Coverly experience the dislocation and fragmentation of their small-town background when faced with the labyrinthine workings of Washington and New York. Both cities at first reveal only noise and disorder. Everywhere there is only the "theatrical atmosphere of impermanence."

Coverly accepts a job as a stock clerk in Warburton's department store and begins taking courses at a computer institute. He falls in love with and marries Betsey MacCaffery, an orphan from northern Georgia, takes a job in the computer field, and is whisked off to Island 93 somewhere near Oahu for nine months to engage in computer work for the army. He returns for a short time to St. Botolphs to console Leander, who is upset and disgraced when the *Topaze* is wrecked in a storm and Sarah decides to transform it into a floating gift shop. On the day of the tea party to open the new shop, Leander had fired a pistol out the window at the gathered crowd and immediately thereafter—the enthusiastic crowd is totally unaware of his actions—sent for his sons, claiming that he is dying.

The further adventures of Coverly reveal the spiritual uprootedness of modern existence. He and Betsey go to live in the prefabricated suburban town of Remsen Park. The place is grim and unfriendly, all the houses are built identically, and both Coverly and Betsey miss the friendliness of the small towns in which they were raised. Betsey invites another couple to dinner, but the husband gets drunk and makes a pass at her. No one shows up for Betsey's birthday party, which she has so carefully planned. She becomes melancholy and distraught and has a miscarriage that same evening. Hating Remsen Park, she returns to Georgia, leaving Coverly sad and alone. He hungers for the security and simple pleasures of St. Botolphs, for the place that has always reflected a state of mind of blessedness and natural order. To him modern life remains a realm of chaotic distractions and absurd incongruities.

Moses's adventures may be more bizarre than Coverly's, but the same spiritual loneliness and fragmentation are apparent. Moses is engaged in secret work for a diplomat in Washington, and in his loneliness beds down with a bandleader's wife. The wife, Beatrice, tells an investigator, when he comes across her in a routine investigation of Moses's background, that Moses has seduced her. This she does in an effort to cling to her frail bonds of respectability, which have long since been loosened. Moses is fired as a security risk.

At a resort, where he has gone to fish after his dismissal from the Washington diplomatic job, Moses rescues a woman who has fallen from a horse. Her lover, a Mr. Charles Cutter, puts Moses immediately on his payroll as a reward for his brave rescue. Cutter lures Moses to New York City, where Moses can attend the Trust Company Bond School, and promises him a rosy and affluent future. Moses receives and reads his father's letter, about the disgrace of the *Topaze*, but ignores his father's request to come to St. Botolph's and forwards the letter to Coverly, who does go to visit Leander. Moses cannot be bothered by his father's "crying wolf" once again about his impending death.

With his profession well under way, Moses pursues his latest love, Melissa, the ward of a distantly related Wapshot, old Cousin Justina, living in Cousin Justina's castle outside of New York City. Justina had been a dancing mistress but then had married a five-and-dime store mogul. Before his death Justina's husband had had Clear Haven, the castle, built from rooms and halls pillaged from the great castles and villas of Europe. This great fairy-tale castle now leaks. Moses comes to visit Melissa. At night he scurries

naked over the castle rooftops to make love to her in
her bedroom. He decides to marry her, and Sarah and
Leander attend the simple wedding.

Moses next desires to get Melissa away from Clear
Haven, ruled penuriously by old Justina, a confirmed
man-hater and grotesque parody of Honora Wapshot.
She buys the newly married couple twin beds. Slowly
Melissa transforms herself into a spinster as if undergoing penitence for her earlier transgressions with
Moses. For no overt reason, she adopts invalidism and
chastity, the very modes Justina has proclaimed for
herself. Justina's hold over Melissa remains mysterious
and unresolved. Finally Moses breaks through these
surreal theatrics of his wife and makes love to her once
again, this time in the greenhouse.

Melissa's former husband, a character who has not
appeared in the novel before, suddenly returns to the
castle, steals all of Justina's jewelry during a huge party
there, and is apprehended when he returns by train to
Grand Central Station. Mr. Dewitt, an art curator, is
summoned to examine the paintings at Clear Haven
and announces that they are all forgeries, another example perhaps of Clear Haven's false pretensions as a
sanctuary for tradition and the past. A fire suddenly
starts in the cellars of the castle and utterly destroys
the entire surreal structure. Justina and friends fly to
Athens. At last Moses and Melissa, as if escaping from
a mental institution, go to live happily ever after in
New York City.

Both Betsey and Melissa have sons, and Honora
surrenders most of her money to them. Moses and
Coverly decide to buy Leander a new boat and return
to St. Botolphs for a weekend. On Sunday of that
weekend Leander attends communion, a surprise to
everyone since he rarely goes to church. On Monday
he goes to the beach:

He waded out to his knees and wetted his wrists and forehead to prepare his circulation for the shock of cold water and thus avoid a heart attack. At a distance he seemed to be crossing himself. Then he began to swim— a sidestroke with his face half in the water, throwing his right arm up like the spar of a windmill—and he was never seen again.

All the local people come to the funeral, and Coverly reads the eulogy at the grave.

The Wapshot Chronicle concludes several years later when Coverly, Betsey, and their son, William, return to St. Botolphs to celebrate Independence Day, that same holiday with which the novel opens. Already that earlier Independence Day has become legend: "Many people would remember . . . when some hoodlum had set off a firecracker under Mr. Pincher's mare." Honora has become an ardent Red Sox fan. Betsey loves the floating gift shop and spends much of her time with Sarah there.

In truth Leander Wapshot is the reigning deity and spirit of *The Wapshot Chronicle*, the Prospero of this insubstantial pageant. It is appropriate that the book ends with his death, for in the modern world there is really no place for this ancient god. It is also appropriate that he wishes the final speech of Prospero from Shakespeare's *Tempest* to be read at his funeral:

Our revels now are ended. . . . These our actors, as I foretold you, were all spirits and are melted into air, into thin air. We are such stuff as dreams are made on, and our little life is rounded with a sleep.

Leander's awareness of the natural world around him springs from his lyric celebration of the sensations that that world has to offer. He feels "that the world has contrived to cheer and delight him. . . . He was easily charmed with the appearance of the world.

How could anything go wrong in such a paradise?"
Proof of this delight shines in his journals, the chron-
icles he keeps. He meticulously records the sights,
sounds, and smells of his life:

Barefoot through autumn night. Heart beating. Remember
every step of the way on bare feet. Sand, thistles. Coarse
and silky grass. Oyster shells and soft dirt. Unwrapped
books outside of town on river path. Read in fading light.
Dusk. . . .

The book is filled with the smells that assail
Leander and the other characters, as if the world can
be best appreciated through inhaling the abundance
of its aromas:

I can smell it now. More savory world then, than today.
Smell of ship's-bread bakery. . . . Perfumery of roasted
coffee floated miles down river. Lamp smoke. Smell of
cistern water. Lye from privy. Wood fires.

Such a method celebrates those experiences of
life that can only be apprehended through our five
senses. When these senses are overpowered by the
splendor and aromas of a summer evening or a forest
stillness, we are momentarily restored to some deep
primordial memory of the world in all its loveliness
and lost innocence. To attempt to treat life otherwise,
in the analytical and calculatedly penetrating pro-
cedures of the modern world—the methods of psy-
chologists, rocket scientists, and computer technicians
—threatens to separate man from the very beauties
and sensations of the natural landscape that nourish
him. In *The Wapshot Chronicle* as the scene moves
away from St. Botolphs and into the cities and suburbia, the smells disappear.

Leander's lyric celebration of nature grows and
flourishes within the traditional boundaries of St.
Botolphs. The natural world, which he celebrates in

the poetic catalogues of his journals, flourishes in or near that New England river town. St. Botolphs generates that state of mind wherein the past lingers on into the present as a reminder of the continuity of all things, of the connections between the present moment and the habits and customs of the past. The traditions of the past and the continuing cycles of the natural seasons complement each other and suggest that sense of permanence in life that simultaneously eludes and underscores men's dreams. It is at such moments, when both the past and natural beauty are evoked, that "a searing vision of some golden age" blossoms in the mind, and man's lost innocence, his sense of awe and wonder, is regained.

Within the boundaries of St. Botolphs there is room for the innocent prying of Uncle Peepee Marshmallow and the old ramblings and ways of Cousin Honora. They are rooted to this place. Honora cannot conceive of living outside "those poignant landscapes against which she has played out most of her life." The natural beauty of the landscape coupled with and fostered by the existence and human dimensions of St. Botolphs contribute to Leander's lyric vision.

No vision of life can be sustained without a particular way of living it. Here again Leander shows the way. He wishes that his sons could "grasp that the unobserved ceremoniousness of his life was a gesture or sacrament toward the excellence and the continuousness of things." Each day must have its ceremony, its ritual. Each change in life—birth, marriage, death—demands its special rite. By continuous and habitual repetition, these rituals give to life an overall sense of meaning and order that it would otherwise lack. This traditional sense of order also helps man celebrate and discover the continuities and beauties of his own life, for once life is organized within tradi-

tional customs, its uncertainties and fears can be somewhat overcome. When this is accomplished, then there
is time to contemplate the precious and beautiful
landscapes and moments of elation around us. Beyond
the St. Botolphs of Leander's vision, the world fragments and crumbles, spins chaotically and absurdly.

Ordinary events acquire a certain extra dimension
throughout the novel because they are treated in a
ritualistic manner. These rituals are often described in
terms of mythological and biblical images as if to
suggest their ancient and lasting qualities. When
Coverly watches a burlesque show at the village fair
in St. Botolphs, it is described as if "the rites of
Dionysus were proceeding." The noise of running
water in a stream suggests "the garbled voice of
prophets." In ancient times, according to an old
legend, Leander was also the name of the lover of
Hero, a priestess of Venus, the goddess of love and
spring. When that Leander drowned one night on his
swim across the Hellespont to be with Hero, she threw
herself into the sea. Venus may in fact watch over the
novel as its ruling female deity, for she is often mentioned in conjunction with the sexuality and often
irrational actions of the women throughout.

Leander's final advice in the novel suggests a
veritable list of ways to approach and lead his way of
life:

Bathe in cold water every morning. Painful but exhilarating.
Also reduces horniness. . . . Avoid kneeling in unheated
stone churches. . . . Fear tastes like a rusty knife and do not
let her into your house. Courage tastes of blood. Stand up
straight. Admire the world. Relish the love of a gentle
woman. Trust in the Lord.

The Wapshots maintain their moral and social prestige
in St. Botolphs precisely because of this sense of de-

corum and ceremony. All three aspects of Leander's vision—the love of nature, the sense of tradition and place, the ceremonial style of life—cohere in the Wapshot name and inheritance and create the central vision in *The Wapshot Chronicle*. Deprived of this vision, life becomes a series of disconnected mishaps leading to nothing but spiritual damnation and personal despair.

Honora Wapshot represents an alternative to Leander's "taste for the grain and hair of life." She represents the strictly spiritual side of the Wapshot legacy. "This childless Matriarch" rules the roost. She is a splendid and grand personage, the keeper of Wapshot respectability, full of pride and impulse, able to do as she pleases because of her ancestral heritage and community role. Innocent virtue, innocent of the vagaries and betrayals of the flesh, accompanies her every movement, throbs in her apprehension of the world, which she feels compelled to judge and set in order. Moral duty thrives in her heart and commands her every step. It also, of course, justifies whatever whim arises in her "gallant and absurd" mind. At the end of the novel she continues to reign triumphantly, as though moral duty will prevail forever.

Leander and Honora Wapshot are clearly the most interesting and most developed characters in the novel. They do appear, perhaps, somewhat sentimentalized in the same manner in which Cheever's vision can be misunderstood as a mere celebration of nostalgic longing for the smells and sights of youth and for a simpler past in a quaint old town. Yet they are rescued from the merely sentimental by their sharp-eyed observations of the natural world and of the human condition. Life is no more easily lived in St. Botolphs than it is in the impersonal suburb Remsen Park. It may appear to have more of a definite shape, more completeness, rounded as it is by a sense of nature, of the past, and of the ceremonial aspects of custom and habit, but in truth it is still subject to the terrors and chaos of any time and age.

Throughout this novel loneliness as a basic human condition is a constant theme. This acute and un-relieved awareness of the pain of isolation and aliena-tion permeates the book. Rosalie, on the beach with her lover before the car crash at the beginning of the novel, cannot, in her own mind, separate the power of love from the power of loneliness. They both seem equally isolating and melancholy. The wreck of his beloved *Topaze* causes Leander to feel a deep sense of loss and loneliness. Such feelings are echoed throughout Betsey's life in Remsen Park. "Through every incident—every moment of her life—ran the cutting thread, the wire of loneliness." Even Honora wonders if the feelings of loneliness that assail her are not closer to the essential spirit of life than anything else. These feelings are summed up best, perhaps, in Cheever's description of a railroad station in the late afternoon:

Any railroad station on Sunday afternoon seems to lie close to the heart of time. Even in midsummer the shadows seem autumnal, and the people who are gathered there— the soldier, the sailor, the old lady with flowers wrapped in a paper—seemed picked so arbitrarily from the com-munity, seem so like those visited by illness or death, that we are reminded of those solemn plays in which it appears, toward the end of the first act, that all the characters are dead.

Disappointment also undercuts all things. This realization helps to keep the Wapshot vision within its mortal perspective. No vision, however sacred and accommodating, can ever hope to relieve such a basic human condition entirely. This darker realization un-derscores all the lyric aspects of the novel. It may account for that dark impenetrable background upon which Cheever's lyric moments of light are projected.

In *The Wapshot Chronicle* the basic pattern underlying most of human experience reveals a paradise lost, the sense that innocence and delight have been lost and corrupted by the intrusion of the modern world and adult desires. In the actual living of life, as suggested by the novel, perhaps the feeling of loss of some recognizable innocence and state of grace is all that we can really know. Perhaps such a lost paradise in truth can only be recalled by a backward glance, a sudden aroma out of the past, a brief moment of remembered time. From this perspective, the feeling of loss, along with loneliness and disappointment, contributes to the basic pattern and sensibility of all human experience. No modern chronicle worth the telling can overlook such forces.

In terms of pure plot *The Wapshot Chronicle* tends to be episodic and disjointed. Too often the book fragments into separate stories and events. Yet the episodic nature of the novel can be defended when each episode is viewed as one more example of Cheever's overall pattern. Thus one episode represents lost innocence, another the absurd rootlessness of the modern world, still another the importance of tradition in St. Botolphs. The more the novel deals with contemporary scenes and events, with the cities and the suburbs as opposed to the older New England landscape, the more episodic the structure of it becomes, suggesting that the very episodic form of the book parallels the fragmented experience of living in a traditionless and disoriented modern society.

The book appears to be more casual in its construction than it really is, not because of its episodic nature, but because of the very unevenness and disparateness of the episodes themselves. For every beautifully contrived and invented episode or scene, there are others that seem strangely disconnected from the rest. It is difficult, even given the pattern of past innocence and present corruption, to view the adventures of Moses, clambering over the rooftops of Clear Haven, and the habits and customs of Leander in St. Botolphs as episodes in the same book. Each may fit the overall theme—the uprooted grotesqueries of modern life as compared with the firmly rooted eccentricities of the old New England village—but the tone and mood of each, the elegiac poetic catalogues of the one and the almost surrealistic, fairy-tale farce of the other, produce such different responses in the reader that it is difficult to see how they can both be confined within the limits of the same book.

There do exist certain stylistic problems that tend to linger after one has read the novel. Many of Cheever's characters appear too sketchily drawn and paper thin. After his well-rounded portraits of Leander and Honora Wapshot, the other characters remain unfinished and unexplored. Too many of them are given the favorite Cheever device of the set speech, as if character could best be revealed or suggested by one long soliloquy. Such a speech does not really suffice as a method of coming to know and understand a particular character in a novel. This remains essentially a short-story device that a novel cannot support.

When Cheever's lyric style reflects or describes a moment of lyric beauty—and this, we have suggested, comes closest to the heart of Cheever's accomplishments as an artist—form and content reflect each other in perfect harmony. The theme is in tune with the manner in which it is expressed. The style, however, does not seem suited to the descriptions of more disturbing themes—loneliness, death, decay—because of

its essentially lyric and comic nature. One continues
to wonder whether or not Cheever tried to make desperation appear delightful or palatable or whether or
not he tried to make the appreciation of delight seem
desperate. The novel literally thins out as it continues.
Only life in St. Botolphs flourishes. Only the older
Wapshots are real and well-rounded characters. The
others seem mere stick figures trapped in a Keystone
Cops comedy, as if Cheever cannot or will not treat
the psychic horrors of modern life (which he mentions)
seriously enough.

The world of the novel may be all too easily and
rigidly patterned in a dualistic manner. The unresolved
battle between flesh and spirit, between Leander and
Honora, Moses and Coverly, falls into place readily.
Similarly the constant contrasts between St. Botolphs
and the modern world, New England and New York,
traditional rituals and comic situations, continue relentlessly. The compelling opposition of past and
present, order and chaos, good and evil, stand out
almost too schematically. In much of the book, however, this somewhat schematic simplicity is overcome
by the emotional complexity of Cheever's vision, the
interlocked feelings of loss, hope, grief, celebration,
and despair. This emotional tone and atmosphere
really rescue *The Wapshot Chronicle* from its own
schematic dualisms.

The poetic catalogues of Leander's journals un-
lock the key to the emotional center of *The Wapshot
Chronicle*. Stylistically and thematically they embody
the heart of the novel. The delight in the natural landscape, the appreciation and celebration of the traditions that have flowered in New England's Puritan and
transcendental atmosphere, and the ceremoniousness
of life that gives shape and order to its incomprehensible mysteries form the method and manner of

Leander's character and writings. Innocence may be lost, the world may be interminably corrupt, and loneliness may be the ultimate state of human affairs, but at least this lyric vision of life will serve to restore man, however momentarily, to his innate sense of delight and decency. Whether such an emotionally charged experience can lead man to ultimate wisdom remains to be seen. Perhaps what begins in delight will end in wisdom.

6

The Wapshot Scandal—"Such Eccentric Curves"

The Wapshot Scandal (1964), which traces the further adventures of the characters we met in *The Wapshot Chronicle*, opens on Christmas Eve in St. Botolphs. Snow is falling. Old Mr. Jowett, the stationmaster, waits for a late train down at the railroad station. As he surveys the village around him, we once again get a glimpse of the people there—the Reverend Applegate with gin on his breath, the carolers preparing to sing, the Tremaines and their rug collection, the Ryders decorating their Christmas tree. Just as the train roars in, old Mr. Spofford, on the way to the river to dump a pillowcase filled with nine kittens, falls into the river himself and drowns unnoticed. The beautifully recreated Currier and Ives scene of the snowy Christmas village is shattered by unnecessary death—an ominous foreshadowing of things to come—and the loud train whistle.

Later in the winter Coverly Wapshot returns to St. Botolphs to visit old Honora. He learns from her that the Wapshot House on River Street, empty now since the deaths of Coverly's parents within two years of each other, is haunted by the ghost of his father, Leander. Coverly decides to spend the night there, awakens at three, and thinks he has seen Leander's ghost. He flees from the premises naked, stops abruptly

81

to pull on his underpants, and dashes to take the next train out of town.

Coverly and his wife, Betsey, are now living in Talifer, a company suburban town founded near a missile site where Coverly works. Betsey hates the town and refuses to have sexual relations with her husband. Her sister, Caroline, who comes for a visit, tells Coverly that Betsey was beaten by a stepfather and that she is no novice when it comes to pain and desperation. Coverly leaves for Denver to think things through but is lonely there and returns to Talifer. He makes love once again to Betsey, despite her continued lack of interest and her loneliness.

Coverly decides, one day, to examine the vocabulary of the poet, John Keats, by using a computer to see what Keats's favorite and most-used words are. Griza, a Polish technician, joins him in this endeavor. The project arouses the enthusiasm of Dr. Lemuel Cameron, the director of the missile site. Cameron instantly wants Coverly on his staff and intimidates him into joining that staff, armed as he is with black eyebrows and unchallenged authority. On a skiing trip to the mountains, Coverly sees Cameron descending on the chair lift, but the authoritarian scientist later tells his friends that he skied all the way down the mountain. Of course, this obvious lie arouses Coverly's doubts about his new boss.

Coverly attends a scientific meeting in Atlantic City with Cameron. He observes the temperate façade these scientists cultivate. Cameron suddenly has to leave the meeting, and in his rush, he leaves his briefcase behind. Coverly finds it, catches the next plane to follow Cameron, but loses it in a spectacular airplane hijacking and robbery. Newspaper headlines proclaim: "Disqualified Pilot Robs Jet in Midair." He returns to Talifer and reports the loss to Cameron, who weeps uncontrollably.

When Coverly loses his security clearance, because news of Honora's criminal indictment for failure to pay back taxes has reached Talifer, he flies to Washington to appeal to Cameron. Cameron's own security clearance gets suspended at a congressional hearing. He is revealed as cold, inefficient, and mad as a hatter. He had locked his son, Philip, in a closet as a boy, and the son has become a drooling, insane invalid. The prosecution brings Philip into the committee room to demonstrate Cameron's heartlessness and inhumanity. Cameron attempts to save face by playing some Bach on his violin, which he has brought along with him, but his career is finished. Back in Talifer, Coverly's security clearance is restored.

Life has not been kind to Moses Wapshot. He has always "had the kind of good looks and presence that sweeps a young man triumphantly through secondary school and disappointingly enough not much farther." He has become "the sort of paterfamilias who inspires sympathy for the libertine" in his exacting standards of suburban decency and decorum. He and his wife, Melissa, are living in one of the elegantly surfaced but spiritually troubled suburbs, Proxmire Manor. Melissa has become ruthless in her greed for pleasure and self-satisfaction, a kind of erotic Venus run amuck. She has become bored, disappointed, and restless. She hears tales of Gertrude Lockhart, the suburban slut, who has seduced and been seduced by most of the delivery men and servicemen who have come to her home to assist her in her losing battle against the stainless-steel machinery of modern conveniences, the spoils of the affluent society.

Back in St. Botolphs, Norman Johnson, an Internal

Revenue agent, appears on the scene to inform Honora that she has never in her life paid federal income taxes. Honora visits Judge Beasely, who advises her to take her money and leave the country, because she is too old to finish up her life in the poorhouse. Desperate and uncertain, Honora starts to hang herself in the attic. But she discovers some pages of Leander's old journals, recounting his affair with a notorious Shakespearean actress, Lottie Beauchamp. She becomes so absorbed in the story that she forgets her suicide attempt. Instead she flees to Naples, after a sad farewell to St. Botolphs. After a lonely and exasperating ship crossing, when she was constantly blowing out the ship's generators with her old-fashioned curling iron, she arrives in Italy as a fugitive. Persistent Norman Johnson finally tracks her down in Rome, shows her the order for her extradition, and she, homesick for St. Botolphs, desires to return no matter the consequences. Her spirit broken, she returns home to die.

Honora's money troubles have immediate effects on the lives of both Moses and Coverly. As we have already noted, Coverly loses his security clearance at Talifer because of her indictment. Moses is so upset he immediately leaves Proxmire Manor to raise $50,000 —he has heavily mortgaged his expected inheritance from Honora—leaving Melissa alone with her fears and desires.

Moses's actions precipitate Melissa's downfall. She awakens in the middle of the night, imagines a thief in the house, catches cold, is rushed to the hospital, and in her fevered state there recognizes the shocking fragility and uncertainty of all mortal life. Shortly thereafter she is attracted to Emile Cranmer, the good-looking, nineteen-year-old grocery boy. She learns later that Gertrude Lockhart, the sensual delight of the suburban servicemen, has hanged herself in her garage. Melissa attends her funeral, overcome even more by the sense of approaching death and the precariousness of life. This fear coupled with her own sexual desires, propels her along the path that leads to Emile.

Emile has become bored with people his own age and looks upon Melissa as a tragic and lonely figure who needs rescuing. Sex of course will provide the magic key to salvation and deliverance. He and Melissa travel to her summer house on Nantucket for the weekend, but the autumnal landscape there is bleak and uninviting. High hopes are blasted by actual experience, although they do revel in each other's flesh. They continue their affair in Boston and New York. She buys him a beautiful ring in Boston and, feeling suddenly guilty, abandons him in New York.

Back in Proxmire Manor, Melissa goes one afternoon to a doctor for an examination and permits him to make love to her. She next seeks out the minister, but he cannot help her and sends her to a psychiatrist, Dr. Herzog, whom she refuses to see. Mrs. Cranmer, Emile's mother, learns of the affair from Emile's boss, Mr. Narobi, the grocer. Mrs. Cranmer sees Emile's ring, and tells Moses what has been going on. Enraged, Moses almost strangles Melissa. From then on he is filled with the meaninglessness of modern existence and wanders listlessly into shabby adulteries of his own.

Melissa wins a trip to Rome in a local contest and departs. Emile becomes a deckhand on the S.S. *Janet Runckle* and sails to Italy. While on board, Simon, a friend, tells him of a male beauty contest to be held on the island of Ladros, off Naples. Emile decides to participate before realizing that the contest winners will be auctioned off to the highest bidders, who have come to take away their erotic prizes to satisfy their own sexual cravings. Miraculously he is bought by Melissa, who takes him to a villa on Ladros where she is living, and their old affair continues. Emile remains boyish and youthful throughout, while Melissa dyes her hair red and spends her time shopping at local markets.

Coverly receives a telegram from Honora, now back in St. Botolphs, urging him to come at once. Everything of hers must be confiscated to help pay for the back taxes. She herself is drinking and slowly dying of deliberate starvation. Approaching death wastes her. Her rites of life, "bold, singular and arcane," are at an end. Coverly is the only member of the family to attend her simple funeral.

The Wapshot Scandal ends where it began—it is Christmas in St. Botolphs. Betsey and her son arrive to spend Christmas in Honora's house, before it is confiscated, and to participate in one of Honora's old customs, inviting people less fortunate than themselves for dinner on Christmas Day. The company arriving for Christmas dinner turns out to be a busload of blind people from an institute. Coverly welcomes them warmly: "They seemed to be advocates for those in pain; for the taste of misery as fulsome as rapture, for the losers, the goners, the flops, for those who dream in terms of missed things." Moses, meanwhile, is also in St. Botolphs but remains curled up with a bottle of bourbon and a jowly widow in a local hotel.

The Wapshot Scandal may very well be Cheever's most inventive novel, may even be his masterpiece, filled as it is with dazzling and memorable episodes and events. Such episodes create the rich and colorful texture of the novel. Honora gets to visit the Pope. A Mrs. Lemuel Jameson has become a legend in Prox-mire Manor because, in refusing to pay a parking

ticket, she has been arrested by the police in her own
bedroom. The male beauty contest on the island of
Ladros is filled with interesting characters and events.
Leander's affair on the beach with the Shakespearean
actress includes an eavesdropping dietician and a
spirited moral rebuke from a hotel proprietor.

The most accomplished and beautifully written
episode in the novel is the Easter egg contest. Emile,
fired from Narobi's store because of his affair with
Melissa Wapshot, goes to work at a supermarket in the
area. Mr. Freeley, the manager, decides to hide a
thousand plastic eggs on Easter Eve in the lawns of
the village, a promotional scheme to increase the supermarket's sales to the local housewives. What follows is
a rollicking farcical tale of Emile's hiding the eggs,
five of them golden and filled with vacations in five
European cities, of Mr. Freeley's being waylaid by a
teenage gang and tied up in an abandoned basement,
and of early-rising housewives discovering Emile on
his egg-hiding rounds. The women rush out into the
street, demanding knowledge of the hidden eggs from
Emile. Mr. Freeley is finally freed from his bonds in
the gang's cellar and released, an ironic comment perhaps on the suburban counterpart to resurrection and
deliverance: "The scene was apocalyptic. Forsaken
children could be heard crying in empty houses, and
most of the doors stood open in the dawn as if
Gabriel's long trumpet had sounded." On Emile's way
home, as he dodges and outruns the howling mob, he
drops the golden egg with the trip to Rome in it on
Melissa's lawn.

Despite the several comic episodes of the book,
the air of *The Wapshot Scandal* is "full of pollen and
decay," and no salvation or deliverance are in sight.
On a screen at the Moonlite Drive-In a woman exclaims, " 'I want to put on innocence, like a bright,

new dress. I want to feel clean again!'" This singular cry echoes throughout the novel, and it cannot be satisfied. As Dr. Cameron decides on one of his lust-quenching trips to Rome, "conduct and time were linear and serial; one was hurled through life with the bitch of remorse nipping at one's hocks. No power of reason or justice or virtue could bring him to his senses." The words of John Keats that come forth from Coverly's computer experiment and are carefully re-arranged sum up the novel's emotional texture best:

> Silence blendeth grief's awakened fall
> The golden realms of death take all
> Love's bitterness exceeds its grace
> That bestial scar on the angelic face
> Marks heaven with gall.

In *The Wapshot Scandal*, the modern world is infected by spiritual sterility, ravaged by constant, unilluminating change, and inhabited by weary, un-enlightened wanderers. Everywhere throughout the novel, "the stranger with a hidden face is always wait-ing by the lake, there is always a viper in the garden, a dark cloud in the west." The world "seemed to be without laws and prophets, and total disaster seemed to be some part of the universal imagination." Every-where the landscape looks the same: "The population of this highway gathered for their meals in a string of identical restaurants, where the murals, the urinals, the menus, and the machines for vending sacred medals were uniform." Even old venerable Honora feels that "her sense of reality, her saneness, was no more inviolable than the doors and windows that sheltered her." Even death is deprived of any sacred sense of real existence.

Homeless hordes of dispirited people roam within and across this contemporary landscape in search of some revelation, some insight into the meaning of this meaningless existence that will never come. They appear to be stranded at a point in time and consciousness, which leads nowhere. Without illumination or a sense of personal fulfillment, the large cast of *The Wapshot Scandal* is doomed to wander endlessly, like a line of prisoners in an eternal chain gang or like unenlightened lemmings heading only for imminent disaster at the edge of the sea. Wandering has so much become the spiritual legacy and physical reality of the modern world that "the sense of life as a migration seems to have reached even into [the] provincial backwater" of St. Botolphs.

Old patterns have collapsed. The only certainty is uncertainty, the restlessness of change and sudden transformations. To Cheever, Americans in particular "seemed set apart by an air of total unpreparedness for change, for death, for the passage of time itself," stranded like fish out of water.

In *The Wapshot Scandal*, Rome becomes the only sanctuary for modern wanderers and fugitives. It is where Honora and Melissa, in their separate agonies, go. The migrations from the new world wash up on the shores of the old. Here is the dead-ended refuge for the modern world, the dispirited haven for modern expatriates, as St. Botolphs had been the traditional haven for the securities and blessings of the past. Dark, decadent Rome replaces St. Botolphs as modern wandering and aimlessness have replaced the traditional sense of place and rootedness.

Much of the imagery of *The Wapshot Scandal* is explicitly Christian, as if Cheever were struggling for some clearer, more easily identifiable design within which to find some meaning in modern times. It is as if the more unstructured and rootless the modern experience becomes in his books, as Cheever explored it, the more structural and schematic his imagery becomes to deal with it. An essential duality has always under-scored Cheever's fiction, but in *The Wapshot Scandal* he attempted to describe and define that light and darkness, good and evil, order and chaos, more ab-stractly, more in terms of a definite and purposeful Christian light, as opposed to a more explicit pagan and meaningless darkness. The structural shape and design of the book seems more calculated and ex-plicitly devised than *The Wapshot Chronicle*.

Cheever himself, by interrupting the objective narrative and writing in the first person in a kind of authorial farewell at the end of the novel, created that final scene in which the village and the church steeple are viewed in terms of the constant Christian struggle between good and evil:

Some time after midnight there is a thunderstorm, and the last I see of the village is in the light of these explosions, knowing how harshly time will bear down on this in-genuous place. Lightning plays around the steeple of Christ Church, that symbol of our engulfing struggle with good and evil. . . .

Despite the calculated use of Christian and bibli-cal imagery, however, the reader cannot be certain that these ancient and traditional images will help him grasp the full dimensions of this restless new world of spiritual and physical wanderers. Perhaps the tradi-tional sense of good and evil may no longer even apply under these radically changed circumstances. Moses may be more in tune with the new world, the shape of the modern abyss: "The brilliance of light, the birth of Christ, all seem to him like some fatuous shell game invented to dupe a fool like his brother while he saw straight through into the nothingness of things." Per-haps the old dualisms of Christian order are breaking down, and no new system of values can be discovered. In his short coda at the end of the novel, Cheever bid farewell to St. Botolphs and all it represented, elegiacally completing the Wapshot saga: "I will never come back, and if I do there will be nothing left, there will be nothing left but the headstones to record what has happened; there will really be nothing at all."

Perhaps this underlying sense of the modern age, this sense of nothingness, had overwhelmed the vitality of Leander's vision, which had been expressed so beautifully and centrally in *The Wapshot Chronicle*. This lack of a lyric center may account for the far less poetic color and texture of *The Wapshot Scandal* and for that book's more streamlined emphasis on situation and event. The smells and natural images of *The Wapshot Chronicle* are strongly muted and all but evicted from the fictional texture of *The Wapshot Chronicle*, as if in the modern world, with all its rush and restlessness, such intimate details and moments can neither be found nor appreciated.

Romantic illusions are constantly deflated in *The Wapshot Scandal*, not savagely so as to destroy them utterly, but gently, comically, to put them in their proper perspective. The heroic or lyric pretensions of the characters and their dreams of a golden past are also undercut both by Cheever's style and by the twists and turns of the plot, awakening the characters and the reader to the darker realities of the present. The style, thus, reflects the very theme of the novel. In this manner the ironic tone of the style operates in much the same way as the comic shape operates. The pain, the delusions, the despair, and the wounded spirit are real, but instead of belaboring them to the point of an adolescent's wail, they are placed within the episodic and often absurdist plot and mild ironies of the novel.

The spirit of *The Wapshot Scandal*, however muted and wary, is also extremely comic and good-natured. The set speeches of some of the characters once again provide social comedy at the same time they reveal the loneliness and despair these people experience. The tone remains sprightly and ironic, as if each episode were admired both for its exterior comic shape—the mad dashes of the Easter egg hunt, the outrageous adventures of Honora's shipboard flight to Europe, the Reverend Applegate's church services —and its interior spiritual truths—Emile's love for Melissa, Honora's expulsion from St. Botolphs, Apple-gate's gin–addled reveries.

Of Proxmire Manor, Melissa feels that "the truth was that eventfulness in the community took such eccentric curves that it was difficult to comprehend." Those eccentric curves describe the shape of *The Wapshot Scandal.* The grim outlook on modern experience remains ever-present, but at the same time the reader can delight in the eccentric curves, the essentially comic shape of the novel. Both shape and vision, form and content, work together, each involving and assisting the other. The comic shape of modern root-lessness, the zigs and zags of often outrageous comic situations, counterpoints the real pain and anguish that such rootlessness engenders. That spiritual chaos and despair counterpoint the bizarre and erratic accidents and incidents of life that suggest "the image, hackneyed and poignant . . . of life as a diversion, a festival." Life is neither all tragic nor all comic but is the result of the interaction of both modes of experience.

In the novel each episode seems almost to be tossed into the path of the others in hopes that some revelation, some moment of recognition and wisdom, may be found. It is as if Cheever has set up these juxtaposed events and waited for their meanings to be revealed in the juxtapositions themselves: disparate incidents placed together could interact together by their very proximity, thus generating new perspectives and insights into the vision that is created.

The wealth of episodes and incidents in *The Wapshot Scandal* assures the reader, or in any case may intimate to the reader, that life may be no mere one-way route to ultimate darkness. The realistic texture of the novel, those objects and observations of Cheever's style, also reveals moments of dazzling hope, lyric beauty, and spiritual grace. These moments, however infrequent in the novel (they provided the essential texture of *The Wapshot Chronicle*) and however overridden by the aspects of contemporary despair, do exist. Such moments cannot endure, just as St. Botolphs and Leander certainly cannot, but they are no less real for their brevity than modern chaos is for its longevity.

The most lengthy moment of illumination and hope in *The Wapshot Scandal* occurs in Cameron's committee hearing when an old man offers his view of the modern situation. His ideas suggest Leander's lyric vision of life:

"Come, come, let us rush to the earth. It is shaped like an egg, covered with fertile seas and continents, warmed and lighted by the sun. It has churches of indescribable beauty raised to gods that have never been seen, cities whose distant roofs and smokestacks will make your heart leap, auditoriums in which people listen to music of the most serious import and thousands of museums where man's drive to celebrate life is recorded and preserved. Oh, let us rush to see this world! They have invented musical instruments to stir the finest aspirations. They have invented games to catch the hearts of the young. They have invented ceremonies to exalt the love of men and women. Oh, let us rush to see this world!"

The man is old. His vision may be an ancient one out of touch with modern existence. He even admits that he was born and raised in a small town, which places him even further from the modern mainstream of urban despair. Yet the stylistic grace and rhythms of this passage suggest all too clearly how close his ideas and beliefs may be to Cheever's own.

Cheever walked a carefully balanced tightrope in this novel, and that tightrope was strung carefully and conspicuously between the opposing poles of human experience: flesh and spirit, good and evil, past and present, life and death, order and chaos. He saw the chasms beneath him—the spiritual sterility, the endless chain of wanderers, the possessiveness of desire and the selfishness of love—while he held fast to the balancing pole in his hands—his ironies, his comic awareness, an essential sense of human dignity no matter how insistent the indignities of situation and event. The comic shape of the novel and the comic tone of the style are balanced by the tragic spirit and feeling of the novel, and both are part of that vision of life that is neither all-comic nor all-tragic but an inextricable mixture of the two. This careful balance may be the triumph of Cheever's fictional art.

7

Bullet Park—"Lethal Eden"

Bullet Park is Cheever's lethal Eden, that suburban landscape that has become the focus of Cheever's fictional world. The ceremonial and nostalgic past of *The Wapshot Chronicle*, represented by such sturdy characters as Leander and Honora Wapshot, was followed by the aimless and rootless present of *The Wapshot Scandal*, represented by Leander's sons, Coverly and Moses. In *Bullet Park* (1969), the suburban scene is once again explored.

The importance of the setting is revealed immediately, for it is conjured up in the opening lines of *Bullet Park* before the actual story begins: "Paint me a small railroad station." The very landscape itself seems to initiate the events that follow. We enter as guests to this suburban scene, arriving on a train with an as yet unnamed passenger. He has come to buy a house in Bullet Park, and once off the train is given a guided tour of the neighborhood by Hazzard, the appropriately named real-estate agent. The pink plush toilet seat cover flying from a clothesline becomes our first talisman, a recognizable emblem of this suburban realm. The railroad station is the doorway to this fabled realm of affluence and ease. We have been ushered into Bullet Park, an opening glimpse of a new but precarious Eden.

This modern realm, as in legendary realms of the past, has its own "tribal elders." These people set the standards and uphold the values of the suburban scene. There are the Wickwires, true "celebrants" of Bullet Park, dedicated to the "good life," which leaves them bruised and bandaged; suburbia has become for them "a sacrificial altar on which they had literally given up some flesh and blood." There are the Ridleys, who treat their marriage as though it were merely an incorporated business venture. There are the Lewellens, who claim their cocktail parties as a tax exemption by including Mr. Lewellen's company's name on their invitations!

There are misfits in Bullet Park, however, eccentric oddballs who cannot or will not conform to the established suburban decorum. Marietta Hammer views Bullet Park as " 'a masquerade party. All you have to do is to get your clothes at Brooks, catch the train, and show up in church once a week and no one will ever ask a question about your identity.' " Grace Harvey seeks money for her husband who has been jailed for helping his son evade the draft. A vagrant in a soiled white scarf in a police station recalls his days with the Cherokee Indians. Harry Shinglehouse one fine morning leaps to his death beneath one of the speeding commuter trains and leaves only one brown loafer behind him.

The main characters in *Bullet Park* are Eliot Nailles and Paul Hammer. Nailles, the figure of order, the monogamist, the conventional and decent representative of Bullet Park, is distinctly different from Hammer, the figure of disorder, the loner, the wanderer outside the realm of Bullet Park. At the beginning of the novel the visitor to Bullet Park, who is being guided by Hazzard, is none other than Paul Hammer come to buy a new house. Hammer's own unusual adventures, before he arrives in Bullet Park, are described in Part Two of the novel. Believers "in the mysterious power of nomenclature," both Hammer and Nailles realize, on being introduced to one another one Sunday in church, that each is in some way intertwined with the other's fate.

The first part of the book deals almost exclusively with Eliot Nailles, yet another example of the rational and decent suburban man. He often praises the suburban life, for he and suburban conventions are inseparable. Nailles manufactures Spang, a mouthwash, to rid the countryside of bad breath. For him, wickedness is associated with bad breath and illness; health is the outward sign of inveterate goodness. Because of this he thinks "of pain and suffering as a principality, lying somewhere beyond the legitimate borders of western Europe." He is pleasantly if antiseptically married, because not to believe in and accept the regulation of monogamy is to surrender oneself to the forces of darkness and death. This suburban ideal of conventional social behavior should be upheld and protected at all times.

Nailles earns the reader's admiration for maintaining a spiritual delight in and a spontaneous connection with the natural world. His attention to weather, for instance, reveals an almost pagan celebration of the natural cycle of the seasons. The ordinary act of sawing old elms in his backyard becomes inseparable from his own religious musings. Such moments remind one of Leander's poetic catalogues in *The Wapshot Chronicle*.

Part One of *Bullet Park* (the book is divided into three separate parts) not only introduces us to Nailles and his milieu; it also explores the relationship between Nailles and his son, Tony. The relationship is not a happy one; it is the weakest link in Nailles's otherwise comfortable chain of being. He and Tony seem distant and far removed from one another, although to Nailles, Tony represents life itself.

The actual plot begins when, for no apparent reason other than a terrible sadness, Tony takes to his bed and refuses to get up. Three doctors come to see him, one with a useless drug, one complete with psychological jargon, and one a specialist in sleep analysis. None is able, however, to rouse Tony from his torpor.

Possible reasons for Tony's withdrawal are suggested. Nailles recalls Tony's difficult birth in unfriendly Rome. He also recalls the time when Nailles threw the television set out into the night, appalled by Tony's addiction to it. Tony's interest in school has eroded steadily, and he is pulled off the football team in order to study French. He off-handedly threatens his French teacher, Miss Hoe, and is hauled to the police precinct, but the officers release him. Coming to Tony's rescue, Nailles can offer no advice or comfort whatever to Tony. Tony even disappears one night and returns with a Mrs. Hubbard, a war widow with whom he has spent the night. The Nailleses are stunned and ask him not to do it again.

The final scene before Tony takes to his bed occurs one night on a miniature golf course where Tony announces to his father that he intends to leave school. Nailles insists that Tony get his diploma first, that there are certain rules of society that must be followed. Tony, who can only rebel against such conventional and uncertain advice, declares that " 'the only reason you love me, the only reason you think you love me is because you can give me things.' " He finally upbraids his father's useless life of peddling mouthwash. Nailles reacts swiftly, swinging his putter at Tony's head. Tony ducks and flees. The next day he refuses to get up from his bed.

In the conclusion of Part One Tony is miraculously saved by a black, self-proclaimed messiah named Swami Rutuola. It is Nellie, Nailles's wife, who first hears of him through her maid and goes to a slum neighborhood to locate his whereabouts. This mysterious founder of the Temple of Light perfurms his rites as a "spiritual cheerleader" in Tony's bedroom and raises him from his inexplicable sadness by means of a series of chants and repetitious incantations. Tony is cured as mysteriously and almost as quickly as he became ill, and the Swami leaves without recompense. The entire experience so unnerves Nailles, however, that he becomes addicted to tranquilizers. Since the doctor who has first given them to him has been arrested for selling illegal drugs—the tranquilizers contain some form of heroin—he must purchase them from a pusher in a Catholic cemetery near the railroad station. Tony is cured, but Nailles becomes addicted. He must get his fix each morning before taking the train out of Bullet Park.

Tony's rebellion, therefore, dies as swiftly as it was born. He has withdrawn from and been rehabilitated to Bullet Park by an elusive wizard of unknown reputation and powers, a magician of words and apparent spells. The resolution of Tony's dilemma, however, if in fact it can be called a resolution at all (Swami Rutuola "saves" Tony almost as easily as Spang destroys bad breath) has not reunited father and son. They remain as separate as before.

Part Two of *Bullet Park* is Paul Hammer's section, and he stands for everything that Eliot Nailles does not. He is the child of an illicit union between a wealthy socialist, Franklin Pierce Taylor, and his devoted secretary, Grace (later Gretchen) Schurz Oxencroft. The very fact of his illegitimacy threatens both organized society and the fabric of suburban

manners within the social and moral boundaries of
Bullet Park. Hammer's very name is the result of sheer
chance. A gardener happened to walk by a window
with a hammer, when names for the boy were being
suggested, and so he was named.

At the death of his grandmother, Hammer becomes a homeless wanderer. Turned away from his
father's home at Christmas, he goes to his mother's
residence in Austria, only to flee her eccentric bab-
blings and prophecies. Unlike Nailles, he is subject to
sudden loves and impulses. The ragged trail of his
existence zigs and zags from hotel room to hotel room
as he searches for some permanent place. Hammer
suddenly seizes upon a room with yellow walls in
Rome as an image of the permanent security he is
seeking. When that room is denied him, he literally
searches the world for one like it. His quest takes him
finally to Blenville, Pennsylvania, where he locates a
similar room in the farmhouse of a Dora Emmison. She
lets him spend the night in the yellow room, and at
once he seems reborn. He dives into the pool at night
behind the house, walks naked in the darkness, and
listens to the sound of rain as if it were the awakening
of a new and purer innocence.

When Dora Emmison is killed on the turnpike in
a fog on her way to a party, Hammer buys the house
and moves in. Schwartz, his delightful cat, leads him to
a gray house in the woods, in which live the perfume
manufacturer, Gilbert Hansen, and his beautiful granddaughter, Marietta. It is the mysterious white thread
on her dress that acts as a magic catalyst on Hammer
and propels him into loving her, another symptom of
his random impulsiveness.

When in Part Two, Hammer is first introduced, he
is alone on a beach in Bullet Park, fleeing from the
obvious advances of a homosexual to the more con-

ventional arms of a family flying a kite. At that moment
he feels as if the very kite line possesses "some extraordinary moral force as if the world I had declared to
live in was bound together by just such a length of
string—cheap, durable and colorless." He scoffs at the
insubstantiality of such a force, longing "for a moral
creation whose mandates were heftier than the delight
of children, the trusting smiles of strangers, and a
length of kitestring." He recognizes such a moral force
in one of his mother's statements on the evils of American capitalism. Declaring that America is " 'a great
nation single-mindedly bent on drugging itself,' " she
suggests to him the possibility of awakening such a
drugged world to the recognition of its own smug self-
certainty by crucifying one of suburbia's own on the
door of Christ Church: " 'Nothing less than a cruci-
fixion will wake the world.' " Hammer decides to offer
up a ritual sacrifice to awaken Bullet Park, and decides to murder Tony Nailles.

In Part Three, Hammer and Nailles meet. Nailles
initiates Hammer into the local fire department. Both
men go off together on a fishing trip. We observe a
serene Nailles in communion with the sacred sound of
a stream, as "giddy laughter, the laughter of silly
girls and nymphs, rang through the bleak spring
woods." Hammer nervously shifts his head, uncertain
within this tranquil terrain. He is already planning the
sacrifice.

In the book's final chapter Hammer is convinced
of the rightness of his mission. He confides, however,
in Swami Rutuola, as if almost wanting to be stopped
in his plan, and Rutuola rushes to tell Nailles. On the
night of the Lewellens' tax-exempt party, Tony is
kidnapped by Hammer, knocked unconscious, and
driven to Christ Church. Nailles rushes to the church,
chain-saws his way inside, and rescues his son, while

Hammer is sitting in a front pew crying. The sacrifice is stopped. Hammer is sent to the State Hospital for the Criminally Insane, and Tony goes back to school. Nailles, however, is still addicted to drugs "and everything was as wonderful, wonderful, wonderful as it had been."

In *Bullet Park*, Cheever has invested the suburban life style with all the trappings of a newly made myth. Rites and rituals help to shape the suburban consciousness. If subscribed to religiously, they promise order, decorum, and a comfortable and comforting morality. The new suburbanites of Bullet Park believe that they can overcome human frailty and weakness if only they can perform these rites faithfully and completely. Nailles's victory over Hammer may suggest the victory of the suburban life over the uncertainties of any other kind, for in all suburban things Nailles is, indeed, the true believer.

Much of the imagery throughout the book suggests the ritualistic aspects of suburban living. A wallet becomes part of "some substructure of talismans." Volunteer firemen participate in "rites" that hint at ageless rituals. The three doctors who come to examine Tony are compared to "suitors in some myth or legend where a choice of three caskets—Gold, Silver and Lead—was offered to the travelers."

Not all the imagery, however, is as benign or decorative. For instance, the empty bottles after a weekend party become "gods in some pantheon of remorse" of "Chinese demons." The 10:48 commuter train becomes Mr. Wickwire's "Gethsemane." Should more be expected of these suburbanites than their bland decency? Should "prophets with beards, fiery horsemen, thunder and lightning, holy commandments inscribed on tablets in ancient languages" be sent among them to awaken them from their complacency?

Is this why the winter landscape suggests "the landscape for some nightmare or battlefield?" Can there be some kind of apocalypse at hand?

Critics have suggested that the book's structure is faulty and lacks the true coherence of a novel. Despite the overall plot involving Hammer and Nailles, the book all too easily fragments into a series of separate incidents as if several short stories had been unsuccessfully strung together. The book moves swiftly and easily from a game of "I Packed my Grandmother's Trunk" to Hammer's plan to murder Nailles's son, as if each from Cheever's point of view was of equal importance. For this reason the reader tends to remember the isolated events in the book as eccentric incidents rather than as scenes specifically arranged and calculated to move the novel and the central plot forward. This episodic pattern finally weakens the main Hammer-Nailles plot, by detracting the reader's attention from it all too often.

Each incident in *Bullet Park* should reflect the sensibility or emotional tone of Cheever's style. That prose style speaks to that sense of the inherent beauty and joy in all things. The style speaks of joy; it is a lyric embrace of the natural world. It glides across the events and episodes in the novel with its own lyric weightlessness. The style seems to triumph over the oddity and calamity of chaotic experience in its own gracefulness.

The problem of *Bullet Park*, though the book still seems to be the most experimental of Cheever's works of fiction and the most carefully created, may be that the novel comes too incandescently packaged. "Incandescently" is a word that is used fondly throughout the book. The graceful style wraps itself around the horrors at the center of this landscape, and the grace survives or transcends these horrors. Tony is "saved" not by revelation or understanding but by a cheerful litany offered freely by the Swami. Tony reacts not to deeds but to words, not to actions but to style. Such a facile deliverance from such a terrible sadness raises questions about the original depths of that sadness. It is Swami Rutuola's style that saves Tony from his numbing despair.

Beneath the surfaces of *Bullet Park*, beneath the stylistic grace of Cheever's tale, seem to lie darker apprehensions, overtones of mystery and blood sacrifice. The confrontation between Nailles and Hammer suggests a darker order of experience than Cheever's style itself creates. Is Hammer's attempted sacrifice of Tony a real attempt to awaken the people of Bullet Park from their comfortable stupor to some deeper spiritual awareness? Or is the incident contrived merely to allow Nailles the heroic act of rescuing his son to prove dramatically his deep fatherly love? Does Hammer exist as a kind of anarchic Old Testament prophet who has come? Or does he exist as a kind of crazed, chaotic psychopath who must be subdued and destroyed by the good, upstanding citizens of Bullet Park so that everything can be "wonderful" once more? The final impact of *Bullet Park* remains defused and uncertain.

Of all Cheever's novels, *Bullet Park* seems to be the most thinly textured. The atmosphere and aromas of *The Wapshot Chronicle* are merely incidental here. The bizarre events and delightful spirit of *The Wapshot Scandal* are subdued here. The forces of good and evil, of life and death, of hope and despair are clearly outlined, if somewhat muddled in the outcome of their clash. It is almost as if Hammer's demise were necessary in order to legitimize and justify the existence of suburbia in Cheever's own mind once again. Suburban order is surely preferable to absolute chaos, but in that simplistic confrontation, what is not?

In *Bullet Park* John Cheever has dealt once again with the suburban phenomenon, the suburban way of life, of our contemporary age. He has treated it comically in his tale of Hammer and Nailles. It is almost as though the style contradicts the substance, as if the lyric touch cannot deal appropriately with the grimmer reality that is suggested. The despair is there, and it is a real despair, but Cheever seems to have gracefully dodged its darker implications. *Bullet Park* closes on an ironic but gracious note of "wonderfulness," as if the book were flooded once again by suburbia's own pretensions and sentimental devotions that had been all too briefly shaken.

In *Bullet Park* the darker vision and the lighter style seem to be at odds with one another, uneasily aligned. Perhaps the very conventions of his lyrical literary style may have prevented Cheever from coming to grips with the more desperate aspects of that vision. Perhaps his own emotional perspective, his own natural delight, may have been unable to take his darker musings seriously enough. He has mastered that suburban vision with the incandescence of his style, but we are left realizing that there lurk other Hammers, other demons to assail us, and no amount of incantation can scare them off.

‿‿‿‿‿‿‿‿‿‿‿‿‿‿‿‿‿‿‿‿‿‿

8

Falconer—"The Invincible Potency of Nature"

The setting of *Falconer* (1977), Cheever's fourth novel and tenth book, comes as a surprise. No longer is suburbia the scene of the action. Instead the novel takes place entirely within the confines of a prison—the Falconer Correctional Facility. Cheever himself taught writing at Sing Sing, the penitentiary in his hometown of Ossining in the early 1970s. Such a place is aptly named in the novel, for the falcon is a bird of prey, capable of being trained to pursue other birds. The name, "falcon," is derived from the very shape of the bird's hooked talons.

The novel begins when Ezekiel Farragut, forty-eight years old, a resident of Indian Hill, Southwick, Connecticut, a professor, another of Cheever's sympathetic and articulate male characters, arrives at Falconer. Stunned and disbelieving, he is ushered forcibly into the prison. He has murdered his brother, Eben, and is presently a heroin addict of long standing. (One is reminded of Nailles's reliance on drugs at the end of *Bullet Park*.) Farragut faces up to ten years for his crime, is processed by the prison staff, and is locked into his cell.

In *Falconer*, Farragut meets the curious characters in his cellblock. There are Chicken Number Two, the famous tattooed man and jewel thief who killed his wife; Ransome, the handsome inmate who murdered his father; the Stone, whose eardrums have been pierced with an ice pick during an organized criminal episode; Bumpo, an airplane hijacker, one of the first; and Tennis, a compulsive tennis player and embezzler. From this criminal crew, Farragut learns the intricate and labyrinthine rules and regulations of prison life, the barbaric and brutal customs that make up a prisoner's daily routine. Alienated from and deserted by his self-centered wife, Marcia, who abandons him to his fate, Farragut turns to Jody, a fellow prisoner, who becomes his homosexual lover. The brutality and loneliness of prison life contribute to the desperate need for moments of sexual release.

Cheever filled his novel with odd and extravagant episodes of prison life. Throughout the novel various prisoners tell their tales about their sad lives, their failed marriages, their robberies and rapes. Prisoners gather at a trough, called the Valley, to masturbate in silence. A cardinal visits the prison to say mass, Jody disguises himself as one of the acolytes, and manages to escape in the cardinal's helicopter at the conclusion of the service. On a hot August day, prisoners are allowed to be photographed next to a Christmas tree, the funds for the procedure provided for by the mother of a dead inmate; the photograph is to be sent to their loved ones. A riot breaks out at Amana, the huge upstate prison known as the Wall (a fictional representation of Attica, perhaps, in upstate New York and the scene of the sensational prison riot in 1972). The inmates of Falconer are carefully watched and sectioned off by the guards to prevent any sympathetic demonstrations. When the Wall is retaken by specially trained police and riot squads, Farragut experiences the collapse of some of his hopes for freedom and retribution, having followed bulletins of the disaster

on an ingeniously contrived radio he constructed himself after all radios were confiscated.

At the conclusion of the novel Farragut manages
to escape. In the interim he has unconsciously overcome his heroin habit. When Chicken Number Two
dies, Farragut climbs into the body sack in which the
corpse is to be removed and hides the actual body in
his own bed. Consequently he is lifted up off the floor
by guards and carried outside. While the guards leave
him momentarily to find a car to drive him away in—
the prison hearse is in for an oil change!—Farragut
cuts his way out of the canvas shroud with a razor
blade and stuffs it with stones. He is suddenly, miraculously free and finds a bus to ride away in. On the bus
a friendly stranger, sensing his plight, offers him a
coat. The transformation of prisoner to free man is
complete, though he may be recaptured at any moment, and the novel ends on his enduring hope: "Rejoice, he thought, rejoice."

Farragut's crime is unprecedented in Cheever's
fiction. It seems to be the culmination of a series of
conflicts between antagonistic brothers and/or brother-
figures. Ezekiel Farragut's murder of his brother, Eben,
occurs when Eben, an alcoholic, belligerent, and self-
righteous fraud, reveals to Ezekiel a family secret:
his father had wanted to have the embryo that was to
become Ezekiel terminated by abortion. Appalled by
this final assault on his fragile sanity and hold on life
itself, Ezekiel attacks his brother with a fire iron. As
he falls Eben strikes his head against the hearth and
dies.

This actual act of fratricide suggests many similar
if less deadly confrontations in Cheever's fiction. One is
reminded of the antagonism between Eliot Nailles and
Paul Hammer, for example. In every instance the clash
occurs between two men who embody antithetical

qualities. One is a sensitive man, who believes in some variety of universal or religious order and is capable of experiencing transcendence from the beauty of the natural world; the other is a boorish man, who believes in a gloomy vision of the world or is himself an agent of disorder and anarchy; he seeks only a kind of self-centered satisfaction for his own physical needs. In each work the more spiritual or optimistic individual triumphs over the more physical or pessimistic intruder. One wonders how much the continuing occurrence of this particular conflict in Cheever's fiction, brought to its bloody fulfillment in *Falconer*, reveals about the nature of the relationship between Cheever himself and his older brother, Frederick.

The Farragut family in *Falconer* clearly resembles the Wapshot clan, although in this novel the family is stripped of any sentimental or romanticized aura. Mr. Farragut's love of nature and fondness for sailing are reminiscent of Leander Wapshot, but Mr. Farragut is painted unsympathetically as a kind of selfish eccentric, one who neglects his sons and frequently threatens suicide. Mrs. Farragut, though full of energy and determination, is bellicose and headstrong. Ezekiel cannot even imagine her as gentle or kind. In fact he praises his family only because they somehow managed to convey to him "some pure, crude and lasting sense of perseverance." On the whole, these "pseudo-Wapshots" without sentiment "were the sort of people who claimed to be sustained by tradition, but who were in fact sustained by the much more robust pursuit of a workable improvisation, uninhibited by consistency." The New England haze of St. Botolphs no longer surrounds these cranky characters or excuses them for their own selfish excesses.

In *Falconer* one returns again and again to the presence of the unusual setting. Falconer Correctional

Facility can claim no apparent kinship to St. Botolphs, Bullet Park, or Proxmire Manor. In jettisoning the suburban setting from this novel, Cheever at a single stroke extricated himself from his own ambiguous feelings toward suburbia, the emotions that lay at the core of the confused and uncertain pattern and texture of *Bullet Park*. No longer does he seem to be celebrating the spurious pastoralism and good life of *New Yorker* suburbanites, all too easily mingling his moments of natural lyricism with the comfortable amenities enjoyed by the suburban upper classes. No longer does he seem to be making an apology for affluence, as if trying to convince us that, yes, even the wealthy suffer the pangs of guilt and the futilities of our own querulous mortality. In his creation of the prison world of Falconer, bleak and deadening as it is, Cheever constructs a truly nightmarish realm, a haunting and haunted place where man's spirit is truly confined and assaulted. Cheever's theme has always been, in a sense, the confinement of the spirit in, and the attempts of the spirit to free itself from, our materialistic modern age, but at last in *Falconer* his setting fully embodies this particular vision.

Cheever's style reflects this change of scene. The language retains its polished elegance, but it is harder, tougher, and crackles with obscenities. In the novel Cheever commented about the rough language used by the prisoners: "Obscenity worked on their speech like a tonic, giving it force and structure." Such a statement can also be extended to include the stylistic triumph of the novel as a whole. Gone is the burnished and self-conscious "incandescence" of *Bullet Park*. The obscene exclamations of the prisoners complement and help to create the ambience of the violent world in which they live.

Falconer is perhaps Cheever's clearest and most

accomplished testament of faith. At the center of his
vision of the world there has always been an essentially
lyric consciousness, a celebration of transcendent moments of the human spirit. These moments have been
linked to the natural beauty of the landscape and to
the spiritual need inherent in man for permanent and
humane values. No matter how dark the day in the
alien prison world, Farragut's sustained faith in the
"invincible potency of nature" and in his own spiritual
strivings does not desert him. In fact these momentary
glimpses of an harmonic and beautiful universe are
all the more powerfully experienced because of their
infrequent but spontaneous appearances amid so bleak
a scene. Farragut's moments of transcendence stand
out in *bas relief* against the cold, barren background of
Falconer. At odd moments Farragut catches glimpses
of a leftover Christmas garland hanging from a water
pipe, of a man feeding crusts of bread to pigeons in
the prison yard, of "the simple phenomenon of light—
brightness angling across the air—[which] struck him
as a transcendent piece of good news." These chance
glimpses restore his faith in human nature and in
man's spirit. Even the prison itself contributes to his
lyrical awareness: "The largeness and mysteriousness
of the place was like the largeness of some forest—
some tapestry of knights and unicorns—where a suc-
cinct message was promised but where nothing was
spoken but the vastness." Even here the suggestion
of certain promises, certain hints of a better and more
beautiful world, come to Farragut in a moment of
spiritual uplift and recognition.

This is no mere romanticizing of pretty scenes.
Farragut believes, as he states in a letter to his bishop,
that "while we are available to transcendent experience, we can state this only at the suitable and ordained time and in the suitable and ordained place. I

could not live without this knowledge; no more could I live without the thrilling possibility of suddenly encountering the fragrance of skepticism." His is a religious impulse, provoked and sustained by his own desire for order and by the occurence of spiritual moments. Such a belief suggests the peace and hopefulness of prayer.

The ambiguous clash between the images of Christian hope and nihilistic despair in *The Wapshot Scandal* no longer exists in *Falconer*. The novel, in fact, is filled with religious symbols and images to support Farragut's vision. In his own mind he associates drugs with the kind of exalted experience churches provide, although he realizes that "to profess exalted religious experience outside the ecclesiastical paradigm is to make of oneself an outcast." He loves the holy eucharist, the litany of prayer and love. Even his escape is described in terms of a resurrection from the dead. His final note of quiet affirmation—"Rejoice, he thought, rejoice"—comes as a virtual statement of faith and belief.

The world of *Falconer* is tough and crude, brutal and violent, but Farragut's vision at the center of this closed and alien place transcends the horror. These lyric glimpses can overcome, however fitfully, the institutionalized regimentation of prison life and, by analogy, of our contemporary age. It is the clearest statement of Cheever's own vision of the world and at the same time his most fully realized novel. Farragut's lyric faith sustains his spirit and shelters his battered soul. It is all in such a terrible world he may possess. It is, as Cheever suggests, more than enough.

9

Cheever's Art

The fictional landscape of Cheever's art includes the social pretensions and moral implications of modern suburbia, the larger patterns of human experience, such as the loss of innocence and the deep spiritual hunger for a golden simpler past, and the discovery of beautiful moments to celebrate within the contemporary wasteland. These themes and ideas occur again and again in the short stories and novels. The way they are organized and detailed reveals the form in which Cheever's fictional landscape is created.

Each episode or incident in the short stories and the novels is like a bead on a string of beads: without the string to connect them, each bead would scatter, and with the string, each bead can be seen as one in a series of beads. The order of arrangement on the string depends upon Cheever's method of selection. What dictates or regulates Cheever's selective arrangement of episodes, his juxtaposition of incidents, is his own sensibility and emotional outlook. As Cheever himself has suggested,

I know almost no pleasure greater than having a piece of fiction draw together disparate incidents so that they relate to one another and confirm the feeling that life itself is a creative process, that one thing is put purposefully upon another, that what is lost in one encounter is replenished in the next, and that we possess some power to make sense of what takes place.[1]

Upon this thinner thread of sensibility, thinner certainly than a sturdy and direct narrative or plot line, are hung the seemingly random episodes of the short stories and novels. Such a method may be over-extended in a novel and better suited to the length of the short story, but such is Cheever's method.

The emotional center or vision of Cheever's fiction remains somewhat elusive. His light, ironic style can cut both ways. On the one hand, he seems to be a romantic, yearning for the good old days of yesteryear, far from the madding crowds of the aimless, tasteless contemporary world. On the other hand, he seems to realize the essential futility and unreality of such romantic notions and seems determined to find mo-ments of beauty within the chaotic and graceless con-temporary world. Cheever conjures up the romantic past, those glimpses of St. Botolphs, for instance, in some of the most beautiful lyric passages in his fiction. At the same time the contemporary world is regarded comically, almost so absurdly and outrageously that it cannot be taken all that seriously. Yet the ironies of the style deflate the nostalgic pretensions of the romantic past and reveal the real spiritual uncertainty and psychic pain of the chaotic present. In either case Cheever's style can both illuminate and avoid the im-plications of the situations he writes about. He seems to want his style to be both disarming and protective at once. He seems, finally, to be celebrating his own ability to find delight in both the romantic past, how-ever false, and the contemporary present, however chaotic.

It is essentially Cheever's encounter with experi-ence that we remember, not the encounter of any one

of his characters, unless there exists a singularly strong
identification between his outlook and a particular
character's, as is true of Farragut in *Falconer*. Cheever
is neither concerned with uncovering the complexities
within a particular moment of experience nor interested in sounding the depths of an episode. His is more
an attempt to translate that immediate experience into
the artistic opportunity to display the lyric gracefulness of his style, to focus the reader's attention pri-
marily upon the encounter between the artist and his
material. In *Falconer*, again, Farragut's outlook does
supersede, in terms of the reader's focus, the author's
own.

Such a method basically reveals a comic rather
than a tragic encounter, in which the reader and the
author are distanced from the painful immediacy of
experience and are directed toward the shape or form
that the author gives to that experience. The characters perform in a specific social setting, modern suburbia. All their private griefs, sorrows, and joys are
enacted in that realm and shaped by it. We can laugh
at the exterior situations that engulf these characters,
and at the same time we can sympathize with their
interior feelings. It is this kind of distanced look—
this focusing on outward incident rather than on in-
ward pain—that provides Cheever with his comic
angle of vision on the foibles of modern suburban life.
It is this essential graceful and comic form of Cheever's
style that shapes our lasting impressions of his art.

Cheever's attitudes toward suburbia remain am-
bivalent throughout. It is no accident that even the
names of his suburban sanctuaries contain both good
and evil aspects: "Shady Hill," "Proxmire [near the
mire] Manor," "Gory Brook," "Bullet Park." Only in
Falconer did he succeed in overcoming these ambiva-
lent attitudes by choosing to write about a prison in-

stead of suburbia. He observed accurately the worms in the suburban apple without deciding that the entire apple was, therefore, spoiled. He realized that the dream of suburban stability and comfort, however decent and valorous to the middle-class mind, is yet a dream, unreliable, transitory, and easily shattered. To think otherwise is to accept illusion. To replace a truly moral consciousness with a mere appreciation of comfort and affluence is to replace man's unending spiritual quest for self-knowledge and self-transcendence with a closet full of dead, unilluminating objects. Cheever's darker tales conjure up the strange powers that objects may have over the unenlightened mind. His lyric tales celebrate those moments of beauty and spiritual illumination that can occur only within the sound moral framework of an ordered and disciplined way of life.

Notes

1. John Cheever, quoted in a review of *Bullet Park* by Annette Grant in *Newsweek*, April 28, 1969, p. 103.
2. 1974 Bulletin of the *National Institute* and *American Academy of Arts and Letters*, p. 110.
3. Walter Clemons, "Cheever's Triumph," in *Newsweek*, March 14, 1977, p. 67.
4. John Cheever, quoted in an interview by Susan Cheever Cowley in *Newsweek*, March 14, 1977, p. 73.
5. John Cheever, quoted in an interview by John Hersey in *The New York Times Book Review*, March 6, 1977, p. 28.
6. Elizabeth Hardwick, "The Family Way," in *The New York Review of Books*, February 6, 1964, pp. 4–5.

CHAPTER 2

1. John Cheever, quoted in an interview with Rollene Waterman in *Saturday Review*, Sept. 13, 1958, p. 33.

CHAPTER 4

1. John Cheever, quoted in "Ovid in Ossining," *Time*, March 27, 1964, p. 69.

119

CHAPTER 9

1. John Cheever, quoted in "Ovid in Ossining," *Time*, March 27, 1964, p. 69.

Bibliography

1. WORKS BY JOHN CHEEVER

The Way Some People Live (New York: Random, 1943).
Contents: "Summer Theatre," "Forever Hold Your
Peace," "In the Eyes of God," "The Pleasures of
Solitude," "Cat," "Summer Remembered," "Of Love:
A Testimony," "The Edge of the World," "Hello,
Dear," "Happy Birthday, Enid," "Run, Sheep, Run,"
"The Law of the Jungle," "North of Portland," "Wash-
ington Boarding House," "Riding Stable," "Survivor,"
"Tomorrow is a Beautiful Day," "There They Go,"
"The Shape of a Night," "The Brothers," "Publick
House," "When Grandmother Goes," "A Border In-
cident," "The New World," "These Tragic Years,"
"Goodbye, Broadway—Hello, Hello," "Problem No.
4," "The Peril in the Streets," "The Sorcerer's Balm,"
"The Man Who Was Very Homesick for New York."
The Enormous Radio, and Other Stories (New York: Funk,
1953). Contents: "Goodbye, My Brother," "The Pot of
Gold," "O City of Broken Dreams," "The Children,"
"Torch Song," "The Cure," "The Hartleys," "The
Summer Farmer," "The Superintendent," "The Enor-
mous Radio," "The Season of Divorce," "Christmas Is
a Sad Season For the Poor," "The Sutton Place Story,"
"Clancy in the Tower of Babel."
The Wapshot Chronicle (New York: Harper, 1957).
*Some People, Places, and Things That Will Not Appear In
My Next Novel* (New York: Harper, 1961). Contents:

121

"The Death of Justina," "Brimmer," "The Lowboy,"
"The Duchess," "The Scarlet Moving Van," "The
Golden Age," "The Wrysons," "Boy in Rome," "A
Miscellany of Characters That Will Not Appear."

The Wapshot Scandal (New York: Harper, 1964).

The Brigadier and the Golf Widow (New York: Harper,
1964). Contents: "The Brigadier and the Golf Widow,"
"The Angel of the Bridge," "An Educated American
Woman," "The Swimmer," "Metamorphoses," "The
Bella Lingua," "Clementina," "A Woman Without a
Country," "Reunion," "The Chaste Clarissa," "The
Music Teacher," "The Seaside Houses," "Just One
More Time," "Marito in Citta," "A Vision of the
World," "The Ocean."

Bullet Park (New York: Knopf, 1969).

The World of Apples (New York: Knopf, 1973). Contents:
"The Fourth Alarm," "The Jewels of the Cabots,"
"Percy," "Artemis, the Honest Well Digger," "The
Chimera," "Mene, Mene, Tekel, Upharsin," "Mon-
traldo," "Three Stories," "The Geometry of Love,"
"The World of Apples."

Falconer (New York: Knopf, 1977).

2. WORKS ABOUT JOHN CHEEVER

Aldridge, John W., "John Cheever and the Soft Sell of
    Disaster." In *Time to Murder and Create* (New York:
    David McKay, 1966).

Auser, C.P., "John Cheever's Myth of Man and Time: 'The
    Swimmer.'" *CEA Critic* 29:18–19, March 1967.

Bracher, Frederick, "A Vision of the World." *Claremont
    Quarterly* 11:47–57, 1964.

Bracher, Frederick, "John Cheever and Comedy." *Critique*
    6:66–77, Spring 1963.

Burhans, C.S., Jr., "John Cheever and the Grave of Social
    Coherence." *Twentieth Century Literature* 14:187–
    98, January 1969.

Chesnick, Eugene, "The Domesticated Stroke of John

Cheever." *New England Quarterly* 44:531–52, December 1971.

Garrett, George, "John Cheever and the Charms of Innocence: The Craft of *The Wapshot Scandal.*" *Hollins Critic* 1(2):1–12, 1964.

Gold, Herbert and David L. Stevenson, eds., *Stories of Modern America* (New York: St. Martin's Press, 1961), pp. 169–93.

Graves, Nora C., "The Dominant Color in John Cheever's 'The Swimmer.'" *Notes on Contemporary Literature* 4(2):4–5, 1974.

Greene, Beatrice, "Icarus at St. Botolphs: A Descent to 'Unwanted Otherness.'" *Style* 5:119–37, 1971.

Hall, James and Joseph Langland, eds., *The Short Story* (New York: Macmillan, 1956), pp. 175–76.

Harmsel, Henrietta T., "'Young Goodman Brown' and 'The Enormous Radio.'" *Studies in Short Fiction* 9:407–8, 1972.

Hassan, Ihab, "Encounter with Possibility: Three Novels by Gold, Cheever, and Donleavy." In *Radical Innocence: Studies in the Contemporary American Novel* (Princeton: Princeton University Press, 1971), pp. 180–202.

Hyman, Stanley Edgar, "John Cheever's Golden Egg." In *Standards: A Chronicle of Books for Our Time* (New York: Horizon, 1966), pp. 199–203.

Kendle, Burton, "Cheever's Use of Mythology in 'The Enormous Radio.'" *Studies in Short Fiction* 4:262–64, 1966.

Rupp, Richard M., "John Cheever: The Upshot of Wapshot." In *Celebration in Postwar American Fiction* (Coral Gables, Florida: University of Miami Press, 1970), pp. 27–39.

For extracts from important reviews of Cheever's works, see:

Curley, Dorothy, Maurice Kramer, and Elaine Fialka Kramer, eds., *Modern American Literature*. 4th ed. (New York: Frederick Ungar, 1969, 1976), vol. 1, pp. 211–16; vol. 4, pp. 94–95.

Dissertations about Cheever's works:

Coates, Dennis E., "The Novels of John Cheever." Duke
    University, 1977.
Gaunt, Marcia E., "Imagination and Reality in the Fiction
    of Katherine Anne Porter and John Cheever: Implica-
    tions for Curriculum." Purdue University, 1972.
Valhouli, James N., "John Cheever: The Dual Vision of His
    Art." University of Wisconsin, Madison, 1973.
Wink, John H., "John Cheever and the Broken World."
    University of Arkansas, 1974.

For a comprehensive bibliography of works by and about
John Cheever, see Dennis E. Coates's forthcoming bibliography in *Bulletin of Bibliography,* 1977.

Index

allusions
   biblical, 66, 102–103
   classical, 9, 63, 74
American fiction, modern,
      10
Ames, Elizabeth, vii, 5
"Angel of the Bridge, The,"
      54–58
Asa Bascomb, 58–60
"Autobiography of a Drum-
      mer, The," 2
awards, received by
      Cheever, viii, 7

Betsey (MacCaffery) Wap-
      shot
   in *The Wapshot Chron-
      icle*, 68, 70–71
   in *The Wapshot Scandal*,
      82
biblical references, use of,
      9, 25, 66, 90, 102–
      103
biographical data, vii–viii,
      1–10
   as it appears in the works,
      2–3, 110
Brigadier and the Golf
      Widow, The, viii, 9

"Brooklyn Rooming House,"
      vii
"Brothers, The," 3
Bullet Park, viii, 8, 95–105,
      111
   compared to *Falconer*,
      107

Cash Bentley, 15–17
characterization, in the
      works, 5, 49–50, 51,
      54
   in *Bullet Park*, 96–97
   in *Falconer*, 109–110
   in *The Wapshot Scandal*,
      75, 78, 79
Charlie Folkstone, 21–23
Cheever, Ben (son), 7
Cheever, Frederick
      (brother), vii, 110
   in the works, 3
Cheever, Frederick (father),
      vii
   in the works, 2
Cheever, Frederico (son), 7
Cheever, John
   birth of, vii, 2
   education of, vii
   honors received by, viii, 7
   illnesses of, 7, 8

Cheever, John (*cont.*)
  personal characteristics
      of, 1–2
  quoted, in interviews, 3,
      8–9, 11, 49, 115–16
  and suburbia, 1, 111, 115,
      117–18 (*see also*
      suburbia)
  teaching career of, viii,
      7, 8, 107
  and Thayer Academy, vii,
      3, 4–5
  vision of. *See* vision,
      Cheever's
  visits Italy, viii, 7; Russia,
      viii, 7
  during World War II, vii,
      7
Cheever, Mary Liley
      (mother), vii
  in the works, 2–3
Cheever, Mary Winternitz
      (wife), vii, 6
Cheever, Susan (daughter),
      7
Christianity. *See* religious,
      the
classical references, in the
      works, 9, 63, 74
comic aspects, in the works,
      49, 50, 94, 117
"Common Day, The," 12–13
"Country Husband, The,"
      viii, 28–33
  awards received by, viii,
      7
Cousin Justina, 69–70
Coverly Wapshot
  in *The Wapshot Chron-
      icle*, 67–80

  in *The Wapshot Scandal*,
      81–83, 84, 86
Cowley, Malcolm, 3, 5, 6, 7
critics, on Cheever, 9–10,
      103
cummings, e. e., 6

"Death of Justina, The,"
      23–28
Dr. Lemuel Cameron, 82–
      83, 93–94
Donald Wryson, 14
dream, use of, 27–28
dualism, schematic, 109–
      110
  in *The Wapshot Chron-
      icle*, 79
  in *The Wapshot Scandal*,
      90

Eliot Nailles, 96–104, 107,
      109–110
Emile Cranmer, 84–87, 92
"Enormous Radio, The,"
      40–43
  popularity of, 40
*Enormous Radio, and Other
      Stories, The*, viii, 9
episodic structure, 41–42,
      103, 108, 115–16
  of *The Wapshot Chron-
      icle*, 77–78
  of *The Wapshot Scandal*,
      92–93
"Expelled," vii, 3, 4–5
Ezekiel Farragut, 107–113

Falconer, viii, 8, 107–113
"Five-forty-eight, The," viii,
      7
Francis Weed, 28–32

Gee-Gee, 20–22
"Goodbye, My Brother," 61–64
    and Frederick Cheever, 3

Hammer. *See* Paul Hammer
Hawthorne, Hazel, vii, 5
Honora Wapshot
    in *The Wapshot Chronicle*, 65–79 passim
    in *The Wapshot Scandal*, 81–92 passim
"Housebreaker of Shady Hill, The," 17–20
Housebreaker of Shady Hill, and Other Stories, The, viii, 9
human experience, the, 94
    chaos of, 26, 36
    Cheever's vision of, 16–17, 20, 23, 28
    and disappointment, 76–77
    loneliness as part of, 76
    and loss of innocence, 20, 76–77, 115
    in the modern world, 88–93, 111, 112, 113
    and renewal, 58, 60, 80
    rootlessness of, 35–36, 37, 77
    and the spiritual, 17, 21, 112–13, 115

illusions, of suburbia, 21, 23, 24, 25, 32, 46, 91, 102
imagery, in the works
    religious, 2, 89–91, 113
    ritualistic, 102
innocence, loss of, as subject matter, 20, 76–77, 115
Irene Westcott, 40–43
Irene Wryson, 13–14
Italy, Cheever visits, viii, 7

Jim Garrison, 12–13
Jim Wescott, 40–43
Johnny Hake, 17–20

Keats, John, references to, in the works, 82, 88

Lawrence Pommeroy, 61–63
Leander Wapshot
    compared to the Farraguts, 110
    journals of, 72, 84
    lyric celebration of, 71–73, 91, 93
    as mentioned in *The Wapshot Scandal*, 81, 84, 87, 91, 93
    sense of tradition of, 73–75
    in *The Wapshot Chronicle*, 65–80, 97
"Life With Father" (television script), viii, 7
Liley, Mary. *See* Cheever, Mary Liley
lyric, the
    in the style, 46, 51, 54, 60, 62–63, 63–64, 78, 91, 103–104, 116, 117
    vision of, 51, 60, 63–64, 71–73, 79–80, 93–94, 103, 112, 113, 116

Melissa Wapshot
    in *The Wapshot Chron-
        icle,* 69–70
    in *The Wapshot Scandal,*
        83–92 passim
middle class, the. *See* sub-
    urbia
Mrs. Garrison, 12–13
modern world, the
    Cheever's vision of, 88–
        93, 111, 116, 117
    the human experience in,
        88–93, 111, 112, 113
    rootlessness in, 35–36, 37,
        77
morality
    Cheever's sense of, 51
    suburban, 19
Moses, 23–27
Moses Wapshot
    in *The Wapshot Chron-
        icle,* 65–80
    in *The Wapshot Scandal,*
        83–90
"Music Teacher, The," 36–
    37

Nailles. *See* Eliot Nailles
narrative devices, 9–10, 28
    authorial interruption, 90
    digression, 26–27
    dream sequence, 27–28
    episodic structure, 41–42,
        77–78, 92–93, 103,
        108, 115–16
    prologue, 25–26
    schematic dualism, 79,
        90, 109–110
Neddy Merrill, 43–47
New Republic (magazine),
    Cheever's stories in,

vii, 2, 3, 5
Newsweek (magazine), vii
    interview in, 8
New Yorker (magazine)
    character of, 6, 111
    Cheever's stories in, vii,
        1, 6
New York Times, interview
    in, 8–9

O. Henry Award, viii, 7
Ossining (New York), viii,
    1, 7, 8, 107
"O Youth and Beauty," 15–
    17

Paul Hammer, 96–97, 99–
    104, 109–110
Peaches, 20–22
prologue, as narrative de-
    vice, 25–26
"Publick House," 2–3

religious, the
    experience of, 2 (*see also*
        the spiritual experi-
        ence)
    imagery of, 2, 89–91, 113
    symbolism of, 113
    See also biblical refer-
        ences
renewal, spiritual, 5, 19, 38,
    51, 58, 60, 64, 80
rhetorical repetition, 4, 64
rhythm, of style, 4, 64
rituals, social
    imagery of, 102
    importance of, 14, 36, 63,
        73–75, 102
romantic longing, suburbia
    as, 16–17, 45, 91

rootlessness of man, 35–36, 37, 77
Rosalie Young, 66–67, 76
Russia, Cheever visits, viii, 7

Sarah Wapshot, 65–67, 70
"Scarlet Moving Van, The," 20–23
"Seaside Houses, The," 37–40
setting, of the works, 9–10, 11, 35, 95, 105, 107
Shakespearean references, 71
short stories, the, 11–33
    collections of, viii, 9
    the darker, 35–47, 118
    form of, 28
    the lighter, 49–64
Sing Sing, 8, 107
social manners, of suburbia, 13, 14–15, 20–21, 22, 24, 49, 97, 102
Some People, Places, and Things That Will Not Appear in My Next Novel, viii, 9
spiritual experience, the
    Cheever's vision of, 5, 8–9, 31–32
    as lyric vision, 51, 64, 72, 79–80, 93–94, 112, 113
    man's need of, 17, 112–13, 115
    and renewal, 5, 19, 38, 51, 58, 60, 64, 80
    and rootlessness, 35–36, 37, 77

suburbia as, 11–12, 16–17, 19, 75–76, 97
suffering as, 21
as theme, 9–10
style, 35, 77–78, 93, 94, 115–17
    the comic in, 50
    dispassion of, 13, 14–15, 36, 39–40, 41–42, 49
    lyric, 46, 51, 54, 60, 62–63, 63–64, 78, 91, 103–104, 116, 117
    precision of, 3–4, 60
    problems of, 78–79, 103–104
    as reflection of content, 13, 54, 60, 63, 78–79, 91–92, 105, 111
    rhetorical repetition in, 4, 64
    rhythm of, 4, 64
    word balance in, 4
suburbia
    ambiguous character of, 19, 23, 33, 47
    Cheever's life in, 1
    Cheever's vision of, 111, 115, 117–18
    as comfort and ease, 16, 43, 54, 102, 118
    illusions of, 21, 23, 24, 25, 32, 46, 91, 102
    morality of, 19
    as romantic longing, 16–17, 45, 91
    as setting, 9–10, 11, 35, 95, 105
    as social manners, 13, 14–15, 20–21, 22, 24, 49, 97, 102

Suburbia (*cont.*)
  spirituality of, 11–12,
    16–17, 19, 22–23,
    75–76, 97
  as symbol, 16
Swami Rutuola, 99, 101,
  104
"Swimmer, The," 43–47
  popularity of, 1
symbolism
  examples of, 23, 57, 113
  religious, 113
  suburbia as, 16
synopses for M. G. M., vii,
  5

technique. *See:* narrative
  devices; style
television scripts, viii, 7
Thayer Academy (Massa-
  chusetts), expulsion
  from, vii, 3, 4–5
themes, 35
  as reflected in the style,
    78–79, 91–92
  suburbia, 9–10, 11–12,
    49
  See also: the human ex-
    perience; the lyric,
    vision of; the spiri-
    tual experience
Time (magazine), viii, 7
Tony Nailles, 97–104

vision, Cheever's, 75, 79,
  105
  of the comic, 49, 50, 94,
    117
  of the human experience,
    16–17, 20, 23, 28

  of life as lyric, 51, 60,
    63–64, 71–73, 79–
    80, 93–94, 103, 112,
    113, 116
  of the modern world, 88–
    93, 111, 116, 117
  moral, 51
  of the spiritual, 5, 8–9,
    31–32
  of suburbia, 111, 115,
    117–18 (*see also*
    suburbia)
"Vision of the World, A,"
  51–54

Wapshot Chronicle, The,
  viii, 8, 65–80, 104
  awards received by, 7
  compared to *Falconer,*
    110
Wapshot Scandal, The, viii,
  8, 81–94, 104
  awards received by, 7
  compared to *Falconer,*
    110, 113
Way Some People Live,
  The, vii, 9
White, Katherine, 6
Winternitz, Mary. *See*
  Cheever, Mary Win-
  ternitz
"World of Apples, The,"
  58–60
World of Apples, The, viii,
  9
World War II, vii, 7
"Wrysons, The," 13–15

Yaddo Writers' Colony, vii,
  5